Blame Changer

Understanding domestic violence

by Carmel O'Brien

Threekookaburras

First published in 2016 by Threekookaburras Pty Ltd

Threekookaburras Pty Ltd Melbourne, Australia

Email: info@threekookaburras.com

Web: www.threekookaburras.com

Cataloguing-in-Publication details are available from
the National Library of Australia trove.nla.gov.au

Family violence — Australia — public opinion
Family violence — Australia — prevention
Victims of Family violence — Australia — Services for
Family Violence —Government policy — Australia
Family Violence —law and legislation — Australia

Dewey number: 362.82920994

ISBN: 978 0 9925394 6 7 (paperback)

Printed by Lightning Source

This book is dedicated to Dorothy Rose, who has inspired so much in my life

Some of the proceeds from the sale of this book will be donated to the Luke Batty Foundation and the Dorothy Rose Fund. These funds support survivors of family violence to achieve safety and reclaim their lives.

Carmel O'Brien is a counselling psychologist. She has spent the past 23 years working with individuals and families who have experienced trauma, violence and related issues. Carmel was the director of clinical services at a Melbourne community agency (Doncare) for 14 years. In that role she managed a large counselling program and developed a suite of domestic violence support programs for women and children. Her special clinical interest is the recovery process from intimate partner violence and she currently works in her own general counselling practice. Carmel is the recipient of a Menzies Award (2009) and the Elaine Dignan Award (2010). She is a Fellow of both the Australian Psychological Society and the Cairnmillar Institute. Carmel lives in Victoria, and has seven adult children.

Contents

CHAPTER NINE

CHAPTER TEN

CHAPTER ELEVEN

CHAPTER TWELVE

CHAPTER THIRTEEN

CHAPTER FOURTEEN

CHAPTER FIFTEEN

RESOURCES

Why write this book?

This book is about domestic violence, specifically it is about men abusing women who are their intimate partners. This is a hot topic at present and because it has been my area of work for a long time, often I am asked questions about it.

The same questions keep coming up.
Some of the questions stem from an interest: Why does he do it? Why doesn't she leave?
Are women just as bad as men?
Some are sympathetic: What can we do about it? How can I help my neighbour/sister/friend?
Some are judgmental: Why do some women attract these types of men?
What's wrong with a mother who stays with an abuser?
Some are alarmingly ignorant: It's because of mental illness, isn't it? Aren't they (often the victims) just very needy people?
And some are downright rude: Some people (the victims again) just don't learn, do they?

My experience

I am a counselling psychologist, and for nearly 25 years I have been working with family violence in its many forms. I have worked as a counsellor with hundreds of individual adults and children, as well as working as a relationship counsellor.

In my private practice I have focused on working with women and children affected by family violence. I have also worked extensively in the community sector: in child protection units, in a women's prison, and in counselling and domestic violence support programs.

I recently left a position in a community agency where I managed a large, general counselling program and built up a suite of programs to assist women and children recovering from domestic violence. This role involved extensive supervision of other counsellors and the provision of training and consultation to other agencies. I have been immersed in this topic for decades and have often heard the same questions and comments.

This book explores the questions that are commonly asked about domestic violence and answers questions that nobody asks, to provide an understanding of this very complex issue.

What this book is

This book is not an academically rigorous book. It does not discuss the results of years of careful university research, although it might refer to some excellent work done by others. It is not a formal examination of different theories, although some theories will be up for discussion. It is not a 'how-to' book for counsellors or domestic violence workers.

Rather, it answers questions frequently asked by people about domestic violence, from the perspective of someone who has been working with this issue for over two decades. It puts into everyday language the violence that women experience at the hands of their male partners, because this is the most commonly occurring family violence situation.

The book will look at theories about why domestic violence occurs and what impact it has. It includes information on how to get help, and how to support someone who needs help.

Finally, it will offer some ideas about how to respond well as an individual and as a community.

A note about the case examples

This book contains many examples and stories of intimate partner violence. All names and circumstances are fictional, but I have learned about the abusive behaviour by listening to real victims. Some stories are an amalgamation of different experiences, although no example has been exaggerated. If you find some of the stories confronting, please be aware that they pale into insignificance compared to the realities survivors face every day.

These examples of abusive behaviour are so often repeated that most behaviour, and even some quotes, have been told to me by more than one woman. While each person's experience is unique, there are many parallels in the motivation and behaviour of those who use violence.

I recall a colleague once asking me, at the end of a busy day, what sort of week I'd had.

I replied: 'I think I have worked out the problem — at least eight of my clients seem to be married to the same man.'

CHAPTER ONE
INTRODUCTION TO DOMESTIC VIOLENCE

There is much discussion about terminology among professionals. The terms 'domestic violence' and 'family violence' are sometimes used interchangeably, and are sometimes seen as completely different.

Both terms are used to describe violence that occurs among people who are related or live together. This includes: child abuse; elder abuse; sibling violence; parents who are abused by their children; violence in step-parenting or same-sex relationships. To include all violence covered by these terms would be the role of a quite different book.

However, controlling behaviour and other types of violence all have similar patterns, and most of this book will apply equally to men and women, and to all kinds of relationships.

This book will concentrate on violence perpetrated on women by the men who are, or were, their intimate partners. Americans call this type of family violence 'intimate partner violence'. The Americans also refer to 'battered women' which is a ghastly term that you will not see in this book again. In this book, the terms 'domestic violence' and 'intimate partner violence' are interchangeable.

This does not mean the book will only talk about adults. The wellbeing of children is inevitably threatened when they have a parent or carer using some form of violence or they are being victimised by someone who should care for them, protect and respect them.

Witnessing family violence is, in some jurisdictions, part of the legal definition of family violence, an acknowledgment that children who witness family violence have had violence committed against them. Some of this impact will be covered, because it is important to the understanding of domestic violence.

The way growing up with violence influences the development of children has important implications not only for them but for the general community, and for the battle to rid the community of violence in the future.

The most important features of domestic violence are:

- It occurs when one partner tries to dominate or control the other, often to enjoy increased privileges such as an unfair share of the couple's resources, gratification of their wants and wishes or a feeling of power and importance.
- The patterns of behaviour are repeated and often escalate in severity over time.
- There are many types of violence, it is not limited to physical violence.
- Victims increasingly fear for their wellbeing or their safety, or their life.
- It has devastating effects on victims, who are mainly women and children.

Victims, survivors and perpetrators

I have spoken to women who object to being named a 'victim' and prefer to be called a 'survivor'. They believe that some people associate a negative connotation with the word 'victim' as if there was something wrong with them for being victimised. Some worry that the word 'victim' implies the person was, or is, powerless.

I have even heard professionals talk about a person 'playing the victim'. Some women's abusive partners accuse them of this very thing.

Most victims spend years actively trying to resist the violence done to them. They may not be able to stop the violence, but they are not merely passive. They do all kinds of courageous and creative things to resist the violence being perpetrated upon them.

Other women are quite comfortable being referred to as victims, and one said to me: 'I was certainly victimised and it was a defining stage of my life. At least the victim of a road accident isn't held to blame for being hurt.'

'Survivor' is another common term, and it usually has a more positive connotation. A woman may see herself as a survivor only when she is away from her dangerous partner, and safe; but it is equally true to see every woman living with violence at home as a survivor.

Many of my clients have preferred the term 'survivor' and this book regards both terms as appropriate.

What shall we call the people who use violence to intimidate and control their partners? They are sometimes called perpetrators, or abusers, and these terms clearly hold them responsible for their use of violence.

Many women do not think of their partners as perpetrators, or do not want to. They still have memories of the man they fell in love with and just want him to stop being hurtful.

Some men can be extremely violent or dreadfully hurtful sometimes and charming or loving at other times. So, while this book will sometimes talk about perpetrators, they may also be simply called partners (or ex-partners).

This book does not assume that women are always the victims of intimate partner violence and that they never use violence against men, or against other women.

On the other hand, in whatever way you read the official statistics about domestic violence they show that women are more likely to be victimised by a current or former intimate partner than men, more likely to be hurt enough to need medical attention, much more likely to be killed, and that the perpetrators are overwhelmingly men.[1]

Men as victims, and people in same-sex relationships?

According to a VicHealth report, 20 per cent of the community believes that women and men are equal perpetrators of violence between partners.[2] This is in spite of Australian Federal Government data finding that the real situation is vastly different.[3]

Even websites that claim that one-in-three victims of domestic violence are men are indicating by default that there are twice as many female victims as men. Debates about statistics can derail a useful conversation about family violence. Those who claim that one-in-three victims of domestic violence are men rely on data that asks people to note when they have behaved badly in a relationship, such as by slapping or shouting at a partner.

Much of this data comes from using a questionnaire called the Conflict Tactics Scale,[4] and similar measures.

This scale measures some types of bad behaviour but does not measure domestic violence. It does not take into account the dynamic in the relationship, such as the patterns of behaviour, any fear or intimidation or any kind of sexual violence. It completely disregards both the context and the impact of intimate partner violence.

It could be argued that it is an indicator that men are twice as likely to behave badly in a relationship, which is also probably not true, but it certainly does not measure intimate partner violence. Such data should not be used in a smoke and mirrors exercise to cloud a shameful reality.

The real figures reveal a more stark disparity.[5] An 11-year summary of domestic violence trends in Victoria to 2010 by the Department of Justice, found nearly 80 per cent of victims were women, and 80-90 per cent of abusers were men.[6] Statistics from finalised protective orders in Victoria, for example, show that even when family violence is included in the data, 80 per cent of victims are women and 80 per cent of perpetrators are men.[7]

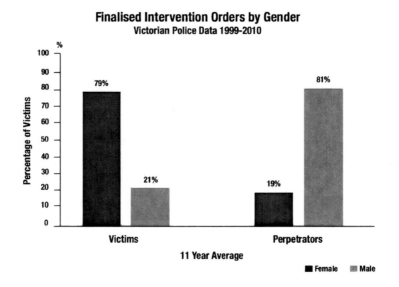

Finalised Intervention Orders by Gender
Victorian Police Data 1999-2010

Women are much more likely to be murdered by a current or former partner than men.

TABLE: Intimate Partner Homicides by Gender 2002-2012 taken from the Australian Institute of Criminology statistics.[7]

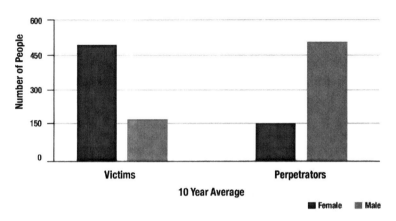

Intimate Partner Homicides by Gender
Australian Crime Data 2002-2012

The Australian Bureau of Statistics Personal Safety Survey 2012 showed that in a 12-month period, fewer than 5 per cent of men who experienced violence were assaulted by a female partner.[8] No one would assume that women are always the victims of intimate partner violence and that they never use violence against men, or against other women.

Men who experience violence are overwhelmingly more likely to be the victims of other men, and much of this violence occurs in one-off situations in public settings.[8]

Women who experience violence are much more likely to be the victims of men, in repeated attacks, behind closed doors.

I make no apology for recognising these facts, and those who do not are destined to remain part of the problem, not part of the solution.

All victims deserve support, and many do not receive it. I recently heard of a male victim being told by a police officer to 'man up'; and a female victim who had been assaulted by her sister being told to 'let things settle, in a couple of weeks you might be best friends again'. This is appalling, and it mirrors the responses experienced by women victims of men's violence since time immemorial. This is why it is important that communities understand family violence and learn to respond in better ways.

Most victims are women, and sharing their journey is my primary area of expertise.

For this reason, this book is about women's experiences as survivors of a range of abusive behaviours perpetrated against them by men.

If you are a man living with a perpetrator, male or female, much of this book will still apply to you.

The behaviour of people who use coercion, abuse and violence to get their way and control others is very similar, whomever they are hurting. This also applies to anyone living with other manifestations of family violence, including intimate partner violence in a same-sex relationship, elder abuse, sibling abuse and the abuse of children.

For anyone living with abuse, taking the first step to seek help to become safe requires all the courage they can muster and requires all the support the community can provide.

Why all this effort?

Why bother trying to solve the problem of domestic violence? Hasn't it always been part of human nature? Don't all relationships involve arguments? If you are in the camp that normalises or minimises domestic violence to this extent, get ready for some challenges to your way of thinking.

There is a simple reason for trying to stop domestic violence — we cannot afford not to. Domestic violence simply costs too much, in human misery and in dollars. One leads to the other, of course. It is estimated that domestic violence costs the Australian economy about $21 billion a year.[9]

That's correct, twenty-one BILLION dollars. This includes lost work days, hospital and medical costs, child protection services, police, legal and incarceration costs, and victim support services (although they get only a very minor proportion of this amount).

In Australia, police are called to incidents of domestic violence thousands of times every week. Yes, that's right, thousands.

In the state of Victoria there are more than 70,000 incidents per year.

Across Australia police deal with more than 650 domestic violence incidents every day. That is about 240,000 a year, or about one every two minutes.[10]

However, police are not called to most incidents. Not only that, we know that women frequently experience more than 30 assaults before they seek help.[11]

The impact on children is enormous, and translates to huge emotional and financial costs into the future.

I think we should try to stop domestic violence just because the human race should behave better than that, but there is no doubt the economic cost to our community is unacceptable.

CHAPTER TWO

WHAT CAUSES THE VIOLENCE?

Many men who do not use violence have said to me: 'I just don't understand it, what's the mentality of these men?'

Men who do not set out to dominate the women in their lives often cannot imagine why a man would behave like this. They can see how it would prevent the possibility of a really loving, successful relationship.

A relationship based on fear is not a recipe for happiness. It damages the person on the receiving end of the abuse, and it also damages the person exerting power. For one thing, a person's very bad behaviour is rewarded by a sense of power and by them getting what they want. If bad behaviour seems to get you what you want, you are likely to repeat it.

In the long run, those who use violence will not have a relationship based on love and support but rather will attract distrust, fear and possibly hatred. True intimacy cannot co-exist with fear. There are many theories put about to explain why men abuse their partners. Some of these are part of the explanation for some men, many of them are nonsense, and some are so victim-blaming they are downright dangerous. The following questions have all been put to me at training or public speaking events. They reflect theories afloat in the community to explain the prevalence of domestic violence.

Do people abuse their partners because of a mental illness?

I once sat in a meeting with the heads of a number of community service agencies. I was there as the local domestic violence expert. I spoke about the nature of a relationship where one partner is controlling; the terror and the psychological damage inflicted on survivors; the wide prevalence; the hundreds of women presenting for help; the sheer nastiness of the perpetrators.

These people, I thought, will understand the problem. I thought they would ask me about the warning signs, how to respond well to disclosures, what services they should offer in their agencies.

The CEO of a community health service was the first to speak, and said: 'Most of the men who do this are mentally ill, aren't they?' Well, actually, they are not. Most of them certainly do not fit the criteria for any mental illness as defined by the psychiatric system in the Diagnostic and Statistical Manual of Mental Disorders (the DSM-V).[1]

The research suggests that only a small percentage of perpetrators would meet the criteria for a mental illness.[1] In fact, people with serious mental health disorders are more likely to be victims of violence, rather than perpetrators. The most common mental health disorders, anxiety and depression, are not associated with a propensity for violence.

To say that a person is abusive because of a mental illness implies that the perpetrator has no choice about their behaviour, and this is simply not the case with almost all mental illness. Let us look at some mental health disorders.

Anti-social personality disorder

Perpetrators of domestic violence are sometimes described as psychopaths or sociopaths, although these are not medical terms. The DSM-V criteria for 'anti-social personality disorder' do list symptoms that match types of behaviour exhibited by controlling or abusive partners.[2]

These include lacking empathy, being egocentric, manipulative, impulsive, deceitful, coercive, callous and irresponsible. If the person is behaving like this to everyone, and has been since a young age, they could be assessed (by a psychiatrist or psychologist) as having this disorder. If they were only behaving like this to their partners and children, they would not fit the criteria.

Narcissistic personality disorder

People who use violence against their partners are also sometimes described as narcissists. The DSM-V criteria for narcissistic personality disorder includes feelings of entitlement, condescension, grandiosity and attention seeking.

They are usually the charming harmers, very good at making a good first impression. I heard one survivor describe her partner as having been a 'honey trap'.

Unfortunately, they are very superficial in their ability to demonstrate empathy in a relationship and are convinced they are better than their partners, if not everyone else. Someone can be narcissistic without having a personality disorder, it is a personality trait like shyness or extroversion, and people who are very narcissistic can be dangerous.

They are often astute and conniving and their main motivation is to win for themselves in a situation, not to have a fair outcome. If that means they need to 'turn on the charm' they will, but they will also be prepared to demolish and humiliate others to achieve their own ends.

In the case of disorders like these, the person is not mentally ill but they generally refuse to comply with social norms, beliefs and expectations. For a diagnosis to be made, they would need to exhibit these traits over many years and in most, or all, situations. This does not mean they have no control over how they behave, but they would need professional help to see the value of consistently behaving in a different way.

Psychotic illnesses

Some mental illnesses interfere with logical thinking because sufferers are plagued by delusions or hallucinations.

These are referred to as psychotic symptoms, such as can occur during some episodes of schizophrenia. Only a small proportion of people who experience mental illness have these symptoms, and when they do the aggression used is usually general rather than targeted only towards their family.

Outsiders can usually notice the aggressive behaviour. If someone is only aggressive to their family, or out of the notice of others, they are clearly making a choice when to be aggressive, and to whom.

Depression and anxiety

The most commonly occurring mental illnesses are related to depression and anxiety. Sometimes, people who behave badly claim they are not responsible because of a mental illness such as depression, but even when someone is depressed or very anxious they are still able to make decisions.

If you kill your partner or child because you have a psychotic delusion that makes you believe they are a horned purple demon who is about to kill the whole family, that is very different from killing your partner or child because you are feeling angry or depressed about the loss of your relationship, especially if your behaviour made it impossible for the relationship to succeed.

Perpetrators of domestic violence usually like to keep their abusive behaviour behind closed doors. In other words, they fully control when, and how, they are abusive.

Victims of domestic violence find it very hard to believe that their partner is really choosing to abuse them, bully them and make their life a misery.

Sometimes, seeing the behaviour as a mental illness can help them come to terms with the fact they still care about their partner, but it is usually a sad misinterpretation of reality.

One of the saddest realisations for someone being abused by a partner is that this is not love, and their partner does not really care about them.

For those asking whether the person using violence towards them is mentally ill, notice how your partner treats other people, such as friends, workmates or family. Are they treating them as badly as they treat you? Can they be charming to others one minute and nasty to you the next?

To summarise, very few people who battle mental illness are violent. Very few people who are depressed are dangerous to others, though some may want to harm themselves at times. Those who have thoughts about harming others have a responsibility to seek help and to do whatever they need to do to keep others safe.

Is it an anger management problem?

Do people abuse others when they are out of control?

Tom and Judy

Judy met Tom when she was 20. Tom was 25, smart, good-looking and very attentive. Judy fell head over heels in love and four months later accepted Tom's proposal of marriage. Things seemed perfect, except that he appeared to be easily offended. He was hurt when her mother thought the relationship was moving too fast. He didn't want certain members of his family invited to the wedding, and then wanted some of her family also not to be invited, the ones he claimed had 'snubbed' him at a family gathering.

Then, one evening when Judy told him they had been invited anyway, at her parents' request (they were, after all, paying for the wedding), he grabbed her guest list and ripped it up, yelled 'obviously his feelings didn't matter,' upended the table and stormed out of the room. Later he told her he couldn't help it, he just 'saw red'. He said this had not happened to him since he was a little boy and that he couldn't help it. He assured her it would not happen again.

I bet you know how this turns out. Tom and Judy married and she lived in increasing unhappiness ever after. Tom lost his temper on the honeymoon when she mixed up the flight times and they nearly missed their plane home. He lost his temper when she told her mother she was pregnant before he got home from work so they could tell her together.

He really lost it when she said she had decided to enrol in a nursing course when their son Nicholas was a year old. One day, Tom went into a rage because the football match he had planned to watch was cancelled. It became standard practice for him to shout at her and Nicholas if they left the light on, or let the cat in, or forgot to bring in the mail.

Judy's life revolved around trying to make sure nothing went wrong, because everything she did was wrong and everything that went wrong was her fault. Eventually Judy realised two things that made her take stock: Nicholas was in trouble for losing his temper at school when he did not get his own way, and her little boy was very scared of his dad.

Judy went to see a counsellor because she wanted to know how to help her son, and asked about how to help her husband with his 'anger problem'. It turned out he only had an anger problem with her and Nicholas.

Even those family members he did not like had never seen him lose his temper. They did not have to experience any of the bad behaviour he visited upon his wife and child.

He had never thrown food at his mother, had never smashed his boss's belongings in a rage, and he did not scream abuse at the policewoman who booked him for speeding. He saved all that for when he was at home.

One night Judy suggested to him that he get some counselling for his anger, and he told her he did not have a temper, that she was just incompetent and impossible to live with.

When she finally told him she wanted to move out, he knocked her unconscious. A few days later she left him and sought help, and it was a long, hard road to safety and relative peace for Judy and Nicholas.

So, Tom is the man who 'saw red' — he thought, or claimed, he could not help it. Notice how he did not get out of control, except with Judy and their young son? As a counsellor, I meet a lot of people who claim they cannot control their angry outbursts.

Closer questioning about particular incidents and relationships shows that they can certainly control themselves. For some reason, they choose not to; effectively giving themselves permission to 'lose it' in certain circumstances, and they usually blame the people they target.

'She makes me mad.'
'She winds me up.'
'She knows I'll lose my temper, she just keeps going on and on.'

Would we accept an excuse such as 'the law knows everyone drinks, so it's just stupid to keep legislating blood alcohol limits that people can't stick to'.

Or 'those shops shouldn't keep putting out shiny new stuff that I want?'

Of course, we would not. We expect people to control their own behaviour.

One of the key messages to understand is that perpetrators make a decision to use violence, it does not just happen.

There are people who use violence habitually and often. The law and the community see this as a choice they have made, and if this behaviour persists, they are likely to be incarcerated. In fact, if the person is so out of control they cannot choose not to use violence, they are too dangerous to be in society.

Road rage is another situation where people sometimes claim they 'lose it'. Talking to 'road ragers' in therapy, they are sometimes surprised to have to admit how many decisions they, in fact, make.

Do they still 'lose it' if their mother is in the car, or their toddler? Would they still 'lose it' if there was a police car alongside? Would they 'show the bird' to an ambulance that cut in front of them? If they got out of the car, what led them to decide to do that? If they assaulted someone, what were they thinking then? In the same way, people who use violence against a partner are making decisions all along the way. For their behaviour to change, they need to understand and admit that they have been making the choice to be abusive, because behavioural change relies on a change in thinking and beliefs.

Is domestic violence due to alcohol and drug abuse?

The belief that alcohol or drugs cause domestic violence, and other violence, is very common. It is true that many perpetrators are affected by alcohol when they are arrested. About half of the domestic violence incidents attended by police include one or both parties being affected by alcohol, and there is some evidence that if the perpetrator has a substance abuse problem the violence will be worse.[3]

Studies indicate that the likelihood of physical violence increases when the male partner drinks or both partners drink.[4] In Australia, women married to men with a drinking problem experience higher rates of violence but this may not be the case in other countries. The link between alcohol and violence seems obvious at first, after all, we know there is an increased likelihood of street violence near nightclubs and hotels.

Thinking a bit further about the role of alcohol in domestic violence raises a lot of challenging questions. What about all those people who get drunk but never hurt or threaten anyone? What about the many perpetrators of domestic violence who do not drink alcohol or use drugs? Why is it that although some women also use violence when they are drunk, problem drinking by female partners does not statistically increase the risk of intimate partner violence? Maybe it's not the alcohol, maybe it's something else.

The thing about alcohol is that it lowers our inhibitions. In other words, when we are drunk we are more likely to take risks, and less likely to think through or care about the consequences of our actions. This is sometimes called Dutch Courage, but is actually Calculated Cowardice, especially in situations of intimate partner violence.

Someone who is unhappy or angry with their partner may decide not to use violence when they are sober, but when they are drunk or drug affected they fail to inhibit their impulse to use violence, and assault their partner.

The first time this happens, the person using violence may be remorseful, but if they do not change their behaviour and seek help if they need it, then the remorse is not genuine. If you have become violent when you are drunk or drug affected you have a responsibility to make sure this does not happen again. People do not become violent just because they drink alcohol, and drinking alcohol does not make people violent.

There is a difference between a contributing factor, an explanation and an excuse. Alcohol may be a contributing factor that increases the likelihood of violence occurring. Being drunk might help explain why you chose to be violent on that occasion. It is not an excuse, and it is reprehensible to expect or demand that you cannot be held responsible.

The bottom line is that if someone is dangerous when they drink, they should not drink. In addition, they should get help to deal with their decisions to intimidate and hurt others. Particularly, they should examine why it is that their partner and their/her children are the primary targets.

I have spoken to many women and children who tailor their lives around their partner's drinking.

'I used to make sure the children were fed and bathed before he came home, so they could go straight to bed if he had been drinking.'

'I could tell by the way he drove into the driveway whether he was sober.'

'My dad was a violent drunk. I can remember him coming in the front door and me running out the back, over the fence and heading hell for leather for my mate's house.'

There are countless biographies written by people whose fathers or stepfathers (or mothers) used violence when they were drunk. The fallout for these children is immense and heart-breaking.

Alcohol is a fuel. No amount of alcohol will start a fire by itself, but if alcohol is added to a fire that is already lit, the fire becomes more dangerous. To systematically abuse one's partner, a person must already have the fire of domination, entitlement or cruelty in their heart.

Education programs that aim to reduce excessive alcohol consumption are no doubt a commendable harm reduction intervention. If they succeed in encouraging people to address the damage they cause when they are violent, or drunk and violent, that is a good thing. Just do not expect that such programs will stop domestic violence — because alcohol does not cause the domestic violence.

Does stress cause domestic violence?

I have heard it said that reality is the leading cause of stress, and certainly stress is everywhere. Everyone has stresses to deal with: everyone experiences losses, grief, sadness, anger, negative changes in their life circumstances, large and small humiliations and demands on their time and resources.

Not everyone is violent, and not all violence occurs when people are particularly stressed. To say that stress causes domestic violence is a bit like saying road rage is caused by driving. Everyone motoring along in a driver's seat is driving, and they all see behaviour by other motorists that they find frustrating, but only a small proportion of drivers decide to verbally or physically assault other motorists.

It might be salutary to try to imagine the stress the average female victim is living with, walking on eggshells, anticipating her partner's every move and mood, trying to make sure every thing in the house is just the way he likes it to be, anticipating how she must act or speak so as not to upset him, wondering how to explain the bruises to her workmates or to her children, never having access to her earnings, being told what money she can and cannot spend, including her own income, cleaning up after the rows, humouring him day and night, and not being permitted to seek support from her own family.

If stress makes you violent, how is it that she is a shy and trembling wreck or a loving and competent mother, rather than violently attacking him and her children?

What about a poor upbringing?

Now, this is an interesting slant on the problem. There is no doubt that many men who use violence did witness it as a child, and when that is the case the person using violence was likely to have been a father or father figure, and the person on the receiving end was likely to have been that child's mother.

Witnessing domestic violence teaches the child where the power lies, and increases the likelihood of a boy becoming a perpetrator of domestic violence as an adult.

However, many men never want to inflict what happened to them as children on to their own family because of their understanding of the pain it caused. Once again, it seems choice is at play.

For girls, growing up with violence increases the likelihood of becoming a victim. But most children who grow up witnessing violence at home, in fact, do not become victims or perpetrators.[5]

Why is this so? What makes the difference? Why is it that although growing up with violence is a risk factor for a number of poor outcomes, many of these children grow up to have happy relationships and be loving and non-abusive parents. Sometimes, I think we should spend less time researching problems and more time researching resilience.

Getting back to those who have grown up with violence at home and become perpetrators, we have to decide whether they are responsible. If someone grows up with a shoplifter, do we excuse them if they also shoplift?

Do we accept the defence that people commit fraud, or murder, or drive when they are drunk because they have grown up with such behaviour and do not know any better, or cannot control what they are doing? Of course not. This is where that difference between an explanation and an excuse is important. Shirley summed up the issue beautifully.

Shirley and Phil

Shirley and Phil came to counselling because they were having problems in their relationship, but said there was no domestic violence. They had been married for 10 years and had two daughters. They were a good team in many ways and made their decisions collaboratively.

There was no power imbalance in this relationship. Phil said he wanted more affection and appreciation. Shirley said she wanted Phil to be less critical and sarcastic. In a way, they wanted the same thing; they wanted to go back to the time when they treated each other with love and respect. Shirley thought she would find it easier to be affectionate if she felt appreciated, too. Among other things, I talked with them about the families they grew up in and what they learned there about relationships and resolving conflict.

Shirley's mum had been depressed and anxious a lot, and often Shirley had to be 'mother' to her younger siblings. Phil remembered his father as always angry and that he was never in his 'good books' no matter what he did. So, Shirley and Phil began the difficult process of rediscovering how to have a positive relationship.

After some early success, as often happens, things started to slip again. Shirley complained that Phil was still rude and critical at times, and that because he had made some efforts to improve he now expected she would forget how hurt she felt. He also admitted he found it difficult to be encouraging of his children, and was often scornful or dismissive of them.

I vividly recall in one session Shirley's response when Phil said (again) that she should understand he couldn't help it, because 'he had a shit time as a kid'.

She leaned towards him and said in a quiet, but strong voice: 'I know, Phil, I know you had a shit time as a kid, but the girls and I are not going to suffer for it anymore.'

It was a turning point, a powerful declaration that Phil had to find a way to deal with his own pain, and not inflict it on his family.

Some people realise that the harm they are causing fulfils their worst fears about growing up to be like their dad and, like Phil, they show a lot of courage in getting help to break this cycle.

Many people will not face their responsibility to stop their violence and they blame their childhood or some other excuse, and the lives of those who love them can become sheer misery, full of danger and despair.

Isn't a lot of domestic violence just a power struggle?

This 'explanation' is sometimes expressed as 'they're just as bad as each other'. There is no doubt relationships do exist where both partners are abusive, but I have learned to be very careful about making this judgment when assessing a situation. First, a person who uses abuse and violence to get their own way or exert illegitimate authority in their intimate relationships will, like any bully, deny or minimise their bad behaviour.

Second, there is research to show that women are more likely to minimise violence and abuse when reporting it to professionals, and that men who report their partners as violent are more likely to exaggerate the violence.[6]

Third, outside observers often get it wrong. The person who seems more 'together' and credible might fool them, or they might just find it hard to imagine a well-mannered person doing such things. Take a look at this research based on police reports.

In the beautiful city of Hobart, a study was made using the records kept on the police data base.[7] Seventy-one randomly selected domestic violence incidents were studied where the woman had been identified by police as the offender.

More than two-thirds (68 per cent) of these women were victims before and/or after their offending incident, and usually with the same partner involved in the current incident.

Also, more than 69 per cent of their male victims were previous and/or subsequent offenders, usually with the partner who was reported as the offender.

The researchers noted that a number of the male 'victims' had used extreme physical violence towards the woman who was arrested.

This included one man throwing the 'offender' to the ground, kicking her several times before hitting her head repeatedly on the bonnet of his car and driving off with the 'offender' on the bonnet.

The police reports included situations where the male victim pulled the female offender out of the car and put her on the ground, and where the (male) victim prevented the (female) offender from leaving.

One report stated that a male reported to be the victim pushed a knife into himself using the offender's hand, and there were several false claims made by these male victims.

The researchers concluded that, in most cases, the female offender was not trying to control the male victim; and, in most cases, the 'victim' did not fear the offender. They also found that reports of subsequent behaviour generally did not reveal any increased risk to male victims.

So, it seems that a large proportion of these women had been acting in self-defence or had not been the aggressor at all, and that even the police can see an incident as much more mutual than it is. One of the difficulties often faced by women in police and court situations is that the context and patterns of abuse go unrecognised.

Not all recurring arguments in a relationship are power struggles. Some are the struggles of one partner to retain some power in a situation where the power imbalance is stark. Some women I have seen in therapy thought they were in a power struggle for years, until they realised that it was a struggle in which they had no power.

Are men just poor communicators?

This is suggested remarkably often — too often. The theory goes something like this: Men are not as good at communicating as women are, and feel out of their depth or frustrated with a woman who can out-talk them, so they resort to violence.

This sounds painfully like the old adage: What's a man to do? Blaming intimate partner violence on poor communication is a dangerous misconception and is wrong for many reasons. Plenty of women, and some couples, seek counselling because they believe this to be the case, or they want to believe it. They think if they improve their communication skills the violence will stop. If one partner is operating to control or punish their partner, communication training will make no difference.

Many men claim to be driven to violence because their partner is badgering, ignorant, demanding, nags them or, as one man told me 'she can talk under wet cement'.

This man told me, 'I have to scare her to get her to stop' — and could not come up with any other option, such as politely stating his case and/or even leaving the room. I asked his wife if he had ever hit her and she said, 'He might as well have.'

Unfortunately, believing this theory allows both parties to think that the victim is at least partly responsible for stopping the abuse. Whether a man uses words, threats or fists to get his message across, his communication is loud and clear.

If he hurts people because he is 'inarticulate' then he can get help to learn better behaviour, but he will find that it is his thinking that is the main problem. Nothing gives him the right to use intimidation or brute force when he's feeling uncomfortable or frustrated. In the meantime, he has a responsibility to do whatever is necessary to make sure he is not a risk to anyone else. Scaring people with whom you wish to communicate is not a valid option.

If your partner becomes abusive when they are losing an argument or they do not want to listen to you any more, then that is an attempt to gain control. It is an abusive tactic to exert control, it is not due to communication problems.

Are some women attracted to abusive men?

Let's get this straight right from the start. People should not abuse one another. They should not abuse workmates, relatives, neighbours, children, old people, gay people, people with a disability or people with different views, incomes or hairstyles.

So, the psychology of the victim is therefore irrelevant to the discussion. Abuse cannot be justified because your partner is weak, stupid, drunk, lazy, soft on the children, late with the dinner or wearing a tight skirt or because they think you are unfaithful.

It is not even justified if you have been unfaithful. Mind you, I have heard all these reasons and a thousand more given by perpetrators to explain their violence.

Becoming a victim of domestic violence has nothing to do with intelligence or education, personality or income. It can happen to anyone, there isn't a 'type'.

It can happen if you are a poor single mother with little education or if you are well-educated, professional or famous. Just ask Rosie Batty, Nigella Lawson or Rihanna Fenty.[8]

A woman does not pick a man to abuse her, consciously or unconsciously, because she is somehow flawed or because she has unresolved issues. Who doesn't?

She meets someone who is appealing, charming and ticks her boxes. He does not advertise his outrageous sense of entitlement or his sexist views or his willingness to use violence; instead he gives her attention, gifts and compliments.

Some men offer to rescue a woman, only to become her next abusive partner. Other factors that can contribute to the chances that a woman can end up being in more than one relationship where she is abused are firstly, the popular notion that possessiveness is a sign of love, and secondly and sadly, there are a lot of men prepared to use violence towards a partner. None of these factors originates within the woman.

While I am interested in the psychological fallout of living with violence and the processes of psychological recovery, that is a different discussion entirely. Meanwhile, the psychology of the victim as an explanation for the violence is irrelevant because the perpetrator is responsible for the violence, not the victim. End of story.

Does domestic violence mostly happen in poor communities?

You can substitute for 'poor' other words like 'ethnic', 'druggie', 'black', or any other discriminatory or derogatory term. In every case, this is wrong.

Domestic violence happens in all social, economic, racial and ethnic groups. The difference is the actions taken by people and where they go for help. People with higher incomes are more likely to go to private doctors or to seek private legal advice or psychological help. People with fewer resources are more likely to ask publicly funded agencies for help, including police. People with higher incomes may be able to find alternative accommodation, they might stay in second homes or with relatives.

Women from low socio-economic backgrounds have fewer options, so they may find it more difficult to leave than those with more resources. They are also more likely to end up in a women's refuge or public housing.

Statistics of domestic violence incidents are often collected from publicly funded agencies, including police data. This means that except for random samples of the whole population (like the National Safety Survey), statistics about intimate partner abuse are often collected from population groups that have few resources other than to go to public agencies for help, so this can sometimes distort the data about the incidence of intimate partner violence in different socio-economic communities.

What happens in well-off homes?

Men who are abusive and controlling often restrict and control the finances; a deliberate strategy to make it impossible for their partners to leave.

A woman with assets or a well-paying job may lose everything, or lose access to her money and have nowhere to go, and they often have a very hard time getting Centrelink benefits or legal assistance.

Financial abuse in higher socio-economic communities is a huge issue, and the level of shame is immense. Government support that is means-tested is usually based on a means test of household income. This is meaningless for a woman who has no real access to the assets or income of her own household.

Penny and Alonzo

Penny and Alonzo lived in an upmarket suburb where prices for real estate were going through the roof. They had both come from comfortable backgrounds, and Penny's parents had paid the deposit on their house when they married 20 years ago.

They enjoyed an affluent lifestyle; they sent their two children to private schools, and enjoyed family holidays around Australia and regular weekends at their beach house. Penny had worked to support Alonzo while he did his MBA and he now earned a high salary as director of his own company.

Penny had endured a lot of abuse in the relationship, including being pushed down a flight of stairs, being almost strangled one day in the family pool and having her head bashed against the dashboard of the car when she asked Alonzo to slow down one evening on the way home from a party.

This last incident frightened her so much she decided to leave the marriage and went to a counsellor to get support with her anxiety and for help in telling her children, aged 16 and 10. She did not think money would be a problem. Then she broke the news to Alonzo.

Many years prior, Penny had become a company director, but knew little about the business. She had signed papers making her a company director, but had done so with little awareness of the liabilities of the role.

In any case, she had never been able to access information or make decisions about the company because Alonzo would not discuss it and answered all queries with, 'leave it to me'.

When she asked him to leave, he did so, to her surprise. He told her he would 'rent somewhere' but it eventually was revealed he had moved into a flat he had purchased years before for his long-term mistress.

Penny soon discovered that Alonzo had emptied the bank accounts and cancelled direct debit payments for all household expenses.

When she enquired at Centrelink about financial assistance she had far too many assets in her name and no record of abuse, as she had never reported any assaults to the police. For months afterwards, unbeknown to her children, there were some weeks when the food in her pantry came from food donated to a local domestic violence agency.

What followed was a harrowing and lengthy battle for Penny's share of the marital assets, and included begging the school to allow the children to remain there until the property settlement was finalised.

A court order was required so joint property could be sold because Alonzo kept refusing to sign any legal documents and it was discovered that Alonzo had borrowed $500,000 on behalf of the company, for which Penny shared liability. This resulted in a legal bill of more than $150,000.

No mention of the abuse was ever made in court; Penny said she did not want her children to find out about it. She was left with enough for a small two-bedroom apartment and two shocked children who were still confused about the break-up of their parents' marriage.

Other groups

There are other reasons why some population groups have a higher incidence of some types of violence, and there are some groups at greater risk of intimate partner abuse.

Women with disabilities, including mental illness, experience family violence at at least twice the rate of women in the general community.

Having a disability can reduce your ability to defend yourself and to escape violence. How can you move out when you need the disability aids built into your house or when your carer is also your abuser?

Indigenous women also experience family violence at much greater rates for complex reasons including dispossession, complex disadvantage and the destruction of culture.

Women in some ethnic and religious communities are more at risk of domestic violence if those communities value men over women or restrict the freedom of women.

Intimate partner violence can occur more in some communities than others, but it is not caused by poverty, ethnicity or colour.

Aren't some men just bad guys?

Some people ask about the psychology of perpetrators. If they are not mad or sad, perhaps they are just bad.

It is tempting and comforting to believe that only nasty, atypical men abuse women and children, physically or mentally. We expect them to stand out in the crowd and at least appear different from other men.

Unfortunately, this is not the case. The partners of my clients have ranged from career criminals to respected professionals, from shopkeepers and tradesmen to professionals and successful businessmen. Some had trouble holding down jobs, others were pillars of their community.

Some had drug habits and some had clerical habits. They come in overalls, business suits and uniforms. They included men who volunteered in their community and took good care of their mothers and helped out their neighbours. Our society has trouble accepting the fact that one individual can be, or can seem to be, so different in different settings.

In 2012, after a public campaign, a Certificate of Merit for Bravery was rescinded when the criminal history of a firefighter was made public.[9] At the time, he was incarcerated for a series of vicious assaults on his former partner.

So long as we believe that only aberrant men practise domestic terrorism, we will not address the prevalence or nature of domestic violence. Neither will we appreciate the link between the status of women generally and the violence perpetrated on some women.

What about men who kill their families?

In the last few years there have been quite a few cases where men have killed their children or their whole family, and the matter has been reported as if they are a 'top bloke' who has been a victim of depression or grief.

Friends and neighbours mourn the loss of these men, and sometimes fail to see the deaths of the children as murder; they seem to view it more as an aberration or a tragedy. It is almost as if these murderers were victims themselves and the horror was unpreventable.

Teacher Jason Lees threw his two-year-old son off Story Bridge in Brisbane and then jumped. Newspapers reported the murder as a 'heartbreaking tragedy'.[10] His headmaster was quoted as saying: 'He was a highly regarded and much loved teacher whose kindness to his students, his gentlemanly approach and enthusiasm for teaching were acknowledged by students, parents and staff alike.'

Geoff Hunt killed his wife, Kim, and their three children before killing himself in Lockhart, New South Wales, in 2014. The press reported:

'Various family witnesses describe Geoff "as hard working, quiet, easy going, warm and loving".'[11]

When Damien Little killed his two children and drove with them off a wharf in Port Lincoln, South Australia, in January 2016, the local football club president was reported as saying: 'You couldn't have asked for a better bloke.'[12]

The good citizens making these judgments are not delusional, they are telling us their experience of those men. A person can have more than one side to their character.

'Top blokes' do not kill their children, flawed blokes do. To deliberately jump off a bridge with your small son or to shoot your own children indicates a sense that you own those children and can dispose of them if you wish.

Some of these men were reported to be depressed or angry, but none were reported to be psychotic. They made a terrible decision. Many more men kill partners and former partners, and not themselves, because they also make a terrible and completely unjustifiable decision.

These are not crimes of passion, they are crimes of possession. Some murdering men have histories of violence or have obvious violent behaviour; some are admired by friends and colleagues, some are both.

This is the difficult truth for non-offending men and women; that ordinary people can be dangerous, that ordinary men abuse their partners.

As well as the more obvious perpetrators who are known to use violence, ordinary men who have good jobs and are contributing positively to their communities may also be monsters at home. These comments from neighbours and relatives of men who have committed horrors on their families prove that you just can't tell. Neighbours are usually surprised that the quiet, law abiding man next door could kill his partner or his child.

Let that sink in. Remember it when you are asking yourself how someone you know got involved with the man who abused her. She couldn't tell either, until it was too late. Remember it when you are tempted to be sceptical when hearing a woman's story of abuse because it does not fit with what you know of her partner. Your experience of that man may be very different from hers.

Causes of Domestic Violence

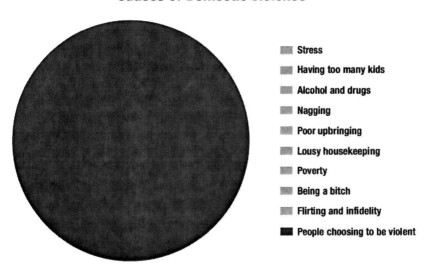

- Stress
- Having too many kids
- Alcohol and drugs
- Nagging
- Poor upbringing
- Lousy housekeeping
- Poverty
- Being a bitch
- Flirting and infidelity
- People choosing to be violent

CHAPTER THREE

WHAT ARE THE WARNING SIGNS?

Domestic violence is about power and control. In every case, one person is trying to dominate and control the other but for the person being controlled and intimidated it is not a power struggle, it is a desperate battle to retain their personal autonomy.

Some women think, especially early in the relationship, that if they are honest and loving and articulate their need to be respected and heard then their partner will see the hurt they are causing and stop.

They may try to demand that their partners show more kindness or respect. Someone who insists on being in control is likely to see this as a threat to his authority and will move to exert more control. They do not become more respectful, they become more manipulative and controlling.

Usually this occurs in such an incremental and insidious way that it is hard to see what is happening. You are like the frog in the well-known experiment where the water you are in is heated so slowly you do not notice, and so you do not jump out before you are cooked.

Are there warning signs?

Not all women talk about noticing warning signs, but many do. Almost invariably they relate to being told what to do, or being told that what they are doing/thinking/saying/planning is wrong.

It is impossible to write a list of all the specific warning signs, but it is easy to name some examples. One woman, who had been shockingly abused, told me that on the first date she had with her partner he had talked her out of ordering the fish dish she preferred and persuaded her to order chicken. Apparently, he wanted the steak but liked to share his dinner date's meal and wanted to try the chicken. This behaviour of 'taking over' became a blueprint for their relationship.

Another woman said her first warning signs were noticing aggravation where it would not normally be expected. She recalled how her partner became unreasonably impatient and sometimes openly surly when he had to wait in a queue.

Julia and Ryan

Julia and Ryan were at school together and fell in love in the year before they finished school. They had plans for their careers, they had fun with their friends and they had families who loved them. The first time there was tension in their relationship was when Ryan wanted to take their physical relationship further than Julia was comfortable with. He gave her lots of reasons why they should have intercourse; it was the natural progression from kissing and cuddling, everyone else did it, he would be gentle, she was just so beautiful he couldn't resist her, and it wasn't healthy to keep stopping at the last minute. When Julia was still unsure his arguments became a bit more insistent. What was wrong with her? Was she a prude? Didn't she mean it when she said she loved him? Couldn't she understand how hard it was for him? 'Come on baby, it's just a natural thing to do.'

One evening he left in a huff and would not return her calls for two days. She was devastated. She did love him, she did want them to be happy, she just didn't feel ready and for her sex was something really special and she wanted to wait a bit longer. In those two days she thought about what he said, she told herself she was being mean to Ryan and that she had obviously hurt him. When they met again, she told him through tears she was very sorry and they consummated their relationship about half an hour later. It wasn't how she had dreamed it would happen, but he was so happy she brushed her disappointment aside.

They left school and went travelling around Australia, they loved the same head-banging music and they went to concerts all over the country. Ryan got a good job and Julia went to university.

So long as Ryan was happy, Julia was happy but the type of scenario that had occurred when Ryan wanted intercourse set the scene for their future relationship, and was played out in a thousand ways over the next few years.

Ryan was the master of manipulative coercion and Julia did her best to please him. They moved to the other side of town even though she wanted to stay close to her family. 'We will visit whenever you want,' he said.

When Ryan's mate had twins he was keen to have children so the children could all grow up 'as cousins'. She had to leave university when they started their family. 'You can always go back later,' he said.

As time went on, Julia began to realise that promises weren't kept and that Ryan's plans and wishes always came before hers. They even sold her car so he could buy a dirt bike to ride with his mates on weekends. It was harder and harder to visit her family as he never wanted to go and she had three children in four years.

At 30, she had still not returned to her studies. Instead, she was working as a checkout operator. Ryan even fell out with his mate who had the twins over some money the mate said he was owed, so the children never did get to grow up 'as cousins'.

When the children were all at school and Ryan had trouble staying employed, Julia decided she wanted to return to university to fulfil her dream of becoming a teacher.

Ryan put up plenty of objections, called her a neglectful 'hopeless shit of a mother' and warned her he would not become 'mummy and daddy' for her by 'looking after' the children while she studied.

Julia failed to be intimidated and told him one evening that she had secured a precious place at uni and had enrolled that day. That was the first time he hit her. It was not the last.

In the case of Julia and Ryan, there were many warning signs, including:

- Ryan's dismissal of Julia's desire to wait before consummating their relationship.
- The techniques Ryan used to coerce Julia into changing her mind, such as making her feel guilty and accusing her of being prudish.

- Refusing to speak to Julia for some days after their first argument.
- Ryan's lack of interest in supporting Julia to fulfil any of her dreams and aspirations that he did not share.
- Ryan's dishonesty in making promises but not keeping them.
- Ryan's persistent behaviour in putting his own wants first, such as selling Julia's car to buy a dirt bike.

Eventually, of course, the violence escalated to overt contempt and verbal and physical abuse.

Some warning signs

Too much, too soon

A common and unexpected warning sign is meeting someone who moves into your life, Hollywood blockbuster style. Being swept off one's feet is such a common memory of many survivors I have met that I always include it on the list of warning signs.

It can be a signal that this new acquaintance is going to expect to be part of your life before you have even had time to assess whether that is what you want. Control has a strong flavour of ownership about it, as we have seen.

Let's say you meet a guy and over the next 24 hours he sends you dozens of texts and wants a commitment from you about a relationship. One woman I know declined a request from a man for a date three or four times. He responded by having flowers delivered to her at work every day until she agreed to go out with him. This is a man who would not take 'No' for an answer.

For a spectacular example of this, there is always the audio online of Dimitri the Stud, in which a man leaves two phone messages for a woman he wishes to date. This audio clip is now used in my domestic violence training courses, so clear are the warning signs in this track.[1]

Swaying your decisions

Giving 'free advice' can seem to be an attempt to be helpful, at least at first.

'Let me take your car to get fixed.'
'I know a better accountant than yours.'
'Why are you still taking those pills?'

Any of this might be part of a normal conversation in a committed relationship but if it is happening very early, you might have met someone who thinks they know better than you do how to control your life.

Abusive partners aim for dominance and there's nothing more controlling than someone who wants to make your decisions for you. Never give up the right or ability to make decisions for yourself because that is a classic marker of abuse from a partner. If you insist on following your decisions, not theirs, check how they react. Unless they are fine with that, you are at risk.

Restricting your social life

A classic warning sign is any attempt to limit who you see or where you go. One common feature of domestic violence is a shrinking of the victim's private life and social contacts. Any attempt to separate you from your friends, family or opportunities is a real worry.

The partner will sometimes come up with a plausible rationale, such as that you are smarter than your friend or that your family doesn't treat you the way you deserve or they want you to spend more of your time with them. They might seem jealous of your social life: 'Why do you want to hang out with them? What's wrong with my company?', or 'So you have more fun with them, do you? I'm not good enough, am I?'

They might accuse you of harbouring a sexual desire for your workmates or friends. Some might try to make their partner feel guilty: 'What am I supposed to do while you're having fun? I've waited all week to be with you. The weekends are our time! You don't care about me.'

Or they might appear to feel inadequate: 'I feel like you're saying I'm not as smart as your friends. I feel like you don't respect me. You think I'm a dud.'

Whatever tactic is used, soon your social network starts to disappear and you start to focus more on your partner's friends and interests, at the expense of being able to maintain your own social network.

Sexual coercion

I nearly called it 'sexual predation' and sexual coercion certainly has an element of predatory behaviour. It can happen to people of any age, and I did meet a 76-year-old woman who revealed she was being pressured by her golf partner for sex. It is even more common among young people and often little understood, partly thanks to a strong popular culture of sexual liberalism.

Putting pressure on someone to have sex or perform sexual acts that they do not want to do is abusive. If someone won't listen to you in this most personal of activities that is a big, red warning flag.

Jealousy

Jealousy and possessiveness are hallmarks of intimate partner violence, and a common and serious form of emotional abuse. Beware of jealous partners, jealousy implies a sense of ownership.

Failure to take personal responsibility

A major warning sign is any failure to take personal responsibility for their actions. Someone who will not pay their way is not only a poor relationship prospect, it indicates that they are likely to not take responsibility for their behaviour.

One woman told me the first time she ever helped out her new boyfriend was when she paid his parking fine because he had given her a story about not having enough money at the time. He never paid her back, of course, and she went on to lose most of her savings and a small inheritance by paying his way, before exiting that relationship. A poor sense of responsibility can be an indicator of a dangerous sense of entitlement.

Demonstrating anger

Anger, like all emotions, is there to both inform us and help us express our feelings. We all need to ensure that in expressing anger we do not harm anyone, including ourselves. Self-control and the capacity to self-soothe is a marker of maturity.

While we may be amused to see a two-year-old having a temper tantrum, throwing toys or screaming and lashing out, it is shocking to see an adult behaving like that. It is also dangerous to those in the vicinity. If your new partner has problems controlling their emotions, especially anger, this is a serious warning sign of future misery.

Discriminatory thinking

Thinking and language that reflects rigid views about the roles of men and women, ideas that men are in some way superior to women, or views that are derogatory about people different from themselves are all danger signs for future abusive behaviour.

A straw poll of colleagues revealed a few examples of warning signs in this category.

'Oh, I never vacuum, that's a woman's job.'

'Don't worry your pretty head about that.'

'You can't trust Indians' ... or Muslims, car salesmen or any other group.

'Well, I bet that stupid idea came from a Labor voter.'

Watch out for prejudice, it goes deep and is hard to unlearn.

Warning signs from their past

One thing we know about human behaviour is that the best predictor of future behaviour is past behaviour.

Change is difficult for us all, especially changes in thinking and behaviour.

We are all, to some extent, ruled by our habits. This is why it is so hard to give up smoking, to change our eating habits or to 'unlearn' an incorrect way of doing a task. It is why parents try to instil in children good manners and study habits, knowing this will make their lives easier later on.

If you meet someone who has behaved badly with other partners this is, unfortunately, a warning sign for their future partners.

Warning signs checklist

These warning signs should make you think carefully about getting any deeper into a relationship.

Too much, too soon

- Assuming a relationship exists before you have made a commitment
- Not respecting your refusal of a request for a date
- Asking very personal questions on early dates
- Giving advice about how you live your life before they really know you
- Planning a future for you together before you have indicated you want a commitment

Restricting your social life

- Objecting to the time you spend with family, friends or interests
- Resenting it when you pursue your own interests
- Suggesting or insisting you stop following your usual activities

Sexual coercion

- Coercing you in relation to sex
- Ridiculing your values
- Trying to get you to make the relationship more physical than you are comfortable with

Jealousy or possessiveness

- Checking on your movements
- Trying to take over your decision making
- Checking your phone or email activity

Demonstrating irresponsibility

- Not paying their share of expenses
- Not apologising when they are wrong
- Overuse of alcohol or drugs

- Minimising, deflecting or otherwise 'not owning' their behaviour, its effects on others or its consequences
- Blaming you for any of their bad behaviour
- Borrowing money and not paying it back, or expecting you to pay for more than your share

Showing anger or violence

- Anti-social behaviour, such as road rage
- Making you worried about what their reaction may be
- Punishing you for infringements of their rules
- Cruelty to animals

Discriminatory thinking

- Attitudes that reflect a belief in gender inequality
- Rigid negative views and prejudices about others
- Rigid, usually antiquated, views about gender roles and the nature of expectations of women

Warning signs from their past

- Poor or fractured relationships with their women relatives
- Having a history of cutting off from people or 'bagging' previous friends or partners

Other warning signs

- Buying you expensive gifts after an incident
- Behaving lovingly one day (or moment), and nastily the next

Now for a more positive story from a young woman of 30.

Raina's story

Raina was doing some internet dating and after meeting one young man for coffee, their next date was a walk in a park on a beautiful summer's day.

They chatted and walked, enjoying the sunshine and learning about each other. Raina mentioned that her friend was expecting a baby. Her new friend looked at Raina's belly button ring and commented, 'Well, you'd have to take that out if it was you.'

She never dated him again; she saw this piece of unsolicited advice as a step too far. As Raina explained it to me: 'He hardly knew me, certainly not long enough for him to be pontificating about my navel.' It may be that this young man thought he was being innocently caring in his remark, but for her a boundary had been crossed.

That, in a nutshell, is the essence of a warning sign. If someone is crossing your boundaries, listen well to your gut feeling. It is better to be sure than sorry, believe me.

Brian and Jill

Brian was quite a good-looking youth, in a mullet and tank top kind of way. He was such a fun party animal and Jill was attracted to his larrikin sense of humour. She thought he had the courage of his convictions and admired how he would argue politics with anyone. She liked how he called her 'sweet baby Jill' and even though he was a big drinker, he was a really funny drunk, playing practical jokes that had his mates in stitches.

He seemed to be smitten with her and after only a few weeks he suggested they move in together. He wanted to be together all the time, and took her with him to all the activities he and his mates liked. He couldn't keep his hands off her and she felt very loved and wanted.

Then one Saturday she had a splitting headache and stomach cramps and said she didn't want to go with him to the races that day, she wanted to stay in bed.

All of a sudden, according to Jill, 'he turned like a tiger' and accused her of being first 'pathetic' and then a 'slut'. She dressed and went with him, feeling sick all day and wishing she had not gone.

Jill and Brian were a couple for 16 years and had two children. Looking back, Jill said she was really only happy for about three months and the occasional good day.

Brian decided how their money would be spent, and there were often arguments about paying school expenses or buying parts for his motorbikes. Brian was mean with money and a bully to the children, but he was so forceful and frightening when he was crossed that she stood up for herself less and less. He swore at her family and discouraged her friends from visiting.

Jill left him on numerous occasions, sometimes it seemed like every other month. She would report him to the police, then withdraw her complaint before any charges went to court. She took out intervention orders, then returned to him within weeks.

He would entice her back with threats or occasionally promises. The promises were rarely kept, but the threats often were. He destroyed her things and terrified their children.

Jill became his punching bag, and said she felt like she was also his 'blow-up doll'. When I asked her what had eventually led her to risk his threats and leave for good, she said it was hearing her 14-year-old daughter sobbing after her dad had called her a 'pathetic slut'.

Did you pick up the warning signs early in this story?

- Wanting Jill to fit into his life, not being interested in fitting into hers
- Reacting with dramatic anger when his day was not going according to his plan
- Deliberately dominating discussions
- Using names for her that suggest she is not as mature as he is
- A lack of empathy when she was sick
- Moving in together very quickly
- Binge drinking/excessive use of alcohol
- Enjoying making fun of others
- Seeing her body as his plaything, to sexually assault at will

Of course, for Jill things went from bad to worse, and so what followed was financial abuse, sexual abuse, physical abuse, threats, intimidation, social abuse, abuse of the children and gross irresponsibility.

This story is a common scenario where there is physical and emotional abuse, which brings us to the next frequently asked question.

How can I tell if I am being abused?

Jane and Steve

Jane left Steve after eight years because he constantly insisted on having everything his own way.

This became abusive when he would ridicule her choices and sabotage her decisions. For example, they talked about and decided to have a dinner party. Jane did a mountain of preparation to make sure the décor, food and music would be just right. She did all the shopping, cooking and table setting and Steve kept putting off the things he had agreed to do, like replace the doorbell, until it was too late for most of them to be done.

'We'll hear them knocking, don't hassle me,' he said.

He did finally mow the front lawn on the afternoon of the party. By that time he was making fun of her efforts, calling her a 'try-hard' and making no effort to keep her beautifully prepared house looking good. He made himself jaffles and left dirty dishes and grated cheese all over the kitchen bench. He let the dog in to walk grass clippings over her clean floors and when she looked upset as she bustled the dog back into the yard and rushed for the vacuum cleaner he commented to the dog, 'Yes mate, now you know how I feel.'

This story shows that there can be a fine line between bad behaviour and intimate partner violence. If this was the worst of Steve's behaviour, you might call him thoughtless, but this was a repeated pattern. For example, he had been so rude to some of her family and friends that they never visited her at home, and so infuriated that she had an important work commitment on his birthday he refused to speak to her for three weeks.

Jane had become afraid of Steve's anger, which seemed to be escalating. By the time Jane left Steve she felt she could not actually live her own life.

Is this violence or is it just bad behaviour? How do we tell the difference? If someone is being physically attacked or blatantly abused the question can be much more easily answered.

Partners behaving badly

At this point some readers may be worried that there are warning signs in their own relationship. There is a difference between intimate partner violence and what I sometimes call 'PBB' – Partners Behaving Badly.

We need to look at different types of behaviour and understand their context. In most intimate relationships there is some bad behaviour, the sort that our mothers might have admonished. Examples would be name calling, slamming doors, refusing to answer questions, or not being completely honest about what our new dress or workbench cost.

It's OK to be angry, and to express that (safely). If this occurs in the context of fundamental mutual respect and leads to a healthy discussion and genuine apology, then that is a healthy resolution to the bad behaviour.

Couples have to learn to resolve conflict if their relationship is to last and grow. They need to learn to accept the olive branches of peace and to renew their love. If these types of behaviour occur in the context of fear, if personal responsibility and apology is absent or if one partner is intimidating the other, then this is intimate partner violence not just bad behaviour. For instance, in many healthy relationships there is some sharing of tasks, and it may be that one partner does more of the household chores, or has the role of organising holidays or buying family presents, mowing the lawn or paying the bills. If this is an agreed division of tasks and both partners feel the outcome is fair then this is not intimate partner violence, provided these decisions are up for free and equal discussion.

The same applies to the issue of personal autonomy, or the ability to make decisions for ourselves. There are many relationships where some negotiation of limits to freedom occurs. For example, one partner might agree to delay their desire to renovate so their partner can take up a course of study, or sell a beloved car so the family can go ahead with that renovation. In a healthy relationship these decisions are made jointly and partners problem-solve together.

However, where there is intimate partner violence the partners are not on equal terms and there will be coercion, threats or simply an executive decision made with little or no discussion. The person who is dominating in the relationship will invariably be the one advantaged by the decision.

CHAPTER FOUR
ASPECTS OF INTIMATE PARTNER VIOLENCE

Domination and control

Domestic violence is characterised by one person trying to control another. This can be done by using physical violence to intimidate or punish the person. It can be a harmful restriction on their daily life. It can mean using the legal system to abuse and demoralise a person after separation. Most tragically, domination and control can end with the murder of women and children. It can be perpetrated by an obvious thug with a history of attacking others, and equally devastatingly by a charming and clever sociopath or a surly introvert.

When one person imposes their will on the other in an intimate relationship, you will find intimate partner violence. As the United Nations' Treaties on Domestic Violence states: Intimate partner violence is an abuse of human rights because it deprives people of their personal autonomy, and that is not something any society should tolerate.[1]

A pattern of behavior

Domestic violence is rarely a one-off occurrence. It is a pattern of behaviour for a specific purpose — the perpetrator wants power in the relationship and control over their partner.

It can begin with what seems to be a one-off occurrence. This is often seen as an aberration and greeted with surprise or shock, and it is not expected to happen again.

Only in time can it be recognised as the beginning of a pattern of abusive behaviour. Sometimes this seems to be a repeating pattern, and survivors become very adept at predicting the individual pattern they have to deal with. Sometimes survivors cannot identify a pattern until they have left the relationship.

One of the perennial issues for women who seek help from police and the law has been that domestic violence incidents are treated as isolated events. The law is designed to respond to, and if necessary, punish discrete incidents: a robbery, a stabbing, a rape, the destruction of property. What if this is the same person attacking the same victim again and again?

In recent times Australia has introduced stalking laws, which recognise a pattern of behaviour. It is time that domestic violence was also recognised in law as a pattern of behaviour that leaves people living in fear and in danger.

The cycle of violence

This diagram illustrates the repetitive nature of domestic violence incidents.

This cycle has been used for decades to help explain intimate partner violence.

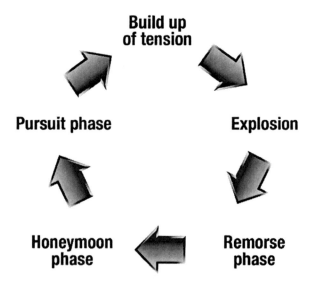

Before we discuss it, let us use the following diagram instead.

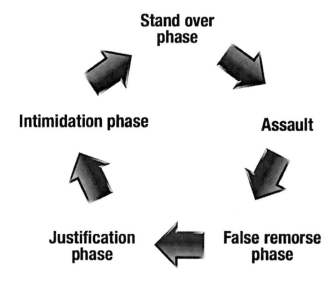

You will notice the language has changed, and the changes are very important so I will explain the thinking behind them. The use of the word 'explosion' creates a feeling that the climax of the cycle is inevitable. This is especially if it comes after the 'build up' phase. I call it the hydraulic view of intimate partner violence. It is also a far too mutual view of intimate partner violence.

The second diagram was developed by my team when I was working at a community agency in Melbourne, Doncare, and was influenced by the work of Alan Wade, from Canada.[2]

You will see that the 'explosion' has been called an 'assault'. This is much less inevitable, and indicates a unilateral act of violence by one person towards another. There is decision making here, with an implied aggressor and victim.

The 'remorse' phase has become the 'false remorse' phase. I have been asked whether this is fair more than once.

'Some men,' I am reminded, 'are really remorseful.'

'Ah, yes,' I say, 'but if the remorse was real, there would not be a cycle.'

If there was true remorse, then the aggressor would have taken whatever steps are necessary to prevent a reoccurrence. If a man is dangerous to live with, he needs to get help. He needs to remove himself from the situation if he is a danger to others. This has to occur even if it means he has to leave his home — until he is safe to live with.

So many people still expect the woman to move out, often with small children, to keep herself safe, so this reversal of responsibility would be just one step to having the person responsible for the violence take responsibility for change.

The 'honeymoon' is meant to describe the phase where the aggressor says they are sorry; in this phase stereotypical behaviour includes buying flowers or jewellery for the victim. What is missing is genuine compassion and an acknowledgement of responsibility.

I cannot figure out how such a description got into a 'cycle of violence' because there are few experiences that are more mutual than a honeymoon. The 'remorse' and 'honeymoon' phases have been replaced with the 'false remorse' and 'justification' phases, which are much more accurate.

Pursuit, promises and justifications are all part of the package in intimate partner violence, and sometimes the victim is also coerced into making promises. If that is the case, then intimidation has started again. The aggressor is in control once more and his behaviour will revert to intimidation, control and his usual manifestations of abuse.

There have always been problems with the cycle of violence to describe intimate partner violence. Many women do not experience a cycle — some men are routinely nasty and manipulative, but they never have a distinct assault phase.

If the cycle of violence seems to fit your experience, you might find that the cycle becomes shorter and assaults or crises more frequent, or you might be with someone who can maintain various phases for months or even years.

If the cycle of violence does not seem to fit your experience, that does not mean you are not experiencing intimate partner violence. If it is helpful, use it, but it does not apply to every situation.

Intimate partner violence comes in many forms

Over many years I have heard innumerable accounts of intimate partner violence. Some types of behaviour are common, such as slapping or ridiculing the victim. Some are bizarre in the extreme. The first time I spoke with 'Amy' — a woman whose partner used to lock her in the car boot to punish her — I was shocked. She talked about lying in the boot of a car from midnight and into the next day, baking in the heat and listening to her small child crying in the house while her husband was passed out drunk inside. I thought she must have been living with a particularly sadistic psychopath.

Since then, nearly 20 years ago, I have heard of at least eight other women who have been subjected to the same appalling treatment. Whenever I think I have heard everything, I hear something new: the same ingredients, but a slightly different recipe.

Domestic violence is often divided into types of abuse: physical abuse, sexual abuse, economic or financial abuse, social abuse, spiritual abuse, emotional and psychological abuse, verbal abuse, cultural abuse, ritualised abuse and legal abuse.

These categories are a good way to outline the vast array of behaviour that can occur in domestic violence.

The downside of this categorisation is that most abusive behaviours fit into more than one category, and some fit into many categories. Take, for example, Amy, the woman locked in the car boot. This was certainly physically abusive, but it was also deprivation of food and water, and of liberty; it was emotional abuse, abuse of their child and it was both punishing and highly controlling behaviour.

On the one hand this could be life-threatening for her and her child, depending on the heat of the day, the length of time and the age and circumstances of the child. On the other hand, it is possible Amy could emerge seemingly unhurt. The psychological and emotional impact of this experience may also differ from person to person. There are many ways to categorise the types of behaviour that occur in intimate partner violence. Most texts list types of abuse like this:

- **Physical abuse:** Includes kicking, punching, choking, pinching, shoving, holding down, and denying medical attention
- **Sexual abuse:** Includes unwanted sexual attention, raping, causing injury to sexual organs, and forcing a person to do sexual acts with him or others
- **Social abuse:** Includes anything that disconnects a partner from their family, friends or social networks such as

embarrassing her in front of friends, and not allowing her to meet people she wants to spend time with

- **Financial abuse:** Includes taking her earnings, making important financial decisions without her consent, borrowing money the partner is liable to pay back without their full consent, commandeering their inheritance, making them account for minor expenses, and deciding how family finances will be spent without free and open discussion

- **Spiritual abuse:** Includes forcing a partner to participate in a certain belief system, or not allowing their partner to participate in their preferred belief system and using religious writings or beliefs to justify abuse

- **Emotional abuse:** Includes put-downs, insults, undermining a person's confidence, using humiliation, using silence and withdrawal as punishment, setting rules they must obey and demanding extreme standards

- **Verbal abuse:** Includes insults, shouting, swearing, name-calling, sarcasm and ridicule, and making derogatory remarks

Sometimes categories such as intimidation and controlling behaviour are added to this list, and many categories overlap each other. Some people have difficulty working out what category of abuse is present in their relationships, and sometimes I am asked which types are 'worse'. There are so many variations within these categories, varying in severity, frequency and outcome, that there is no meaningful answer to that question.

Fear and shame

A feature of intimate partner violence is the fear created by the perpetrator — fear is usually the most powerful way the perpetrator has of controlling his victim.

Fear is the main reason women give for NOT leaving their abusive partner. There are countless soul-destroying ways that fear can be created and maintained. Some are clearly understandable such as fists and weapons, other means can be as subtle as looks or gestures. Fear can be created by hurting or threatening children, pets and family or by destroying property. Just living with an unpredictably angry person who is much bigger and stronger than you is often more than enough to be fearful.

Some women are kept under hostage-like control with the threat that the abuse will be made public or they could lose their lifestyle. For some women, a threat such as, 'If you leave, the children will all have to leave their private schools' can be enough to frighten her into putting up with years of degradation and emotional abuse.

It is not uncommon for women to believe that they are doing the best for their family by putting up with abuse. Many women try to hide it from their children, family or community in the hope it will stop, and to avoid them being affected by scandal and shame.

They are prioritising what they see as the needs of their children or others before themselves. This is not some kind of false martyrdom, it is behaviour that is usually seen as the highest form of courage, sacrificing your own needs and safety for others. In hindsight, it may not have the outcomes that were hoped for, but it should be recognised for what it is.

Domestic violence still carries the stigma of shame for victims as much as perpetrators — sometimes even more so — and keeping it a secret can seem very important. I have seen many women who have stayed with a partner who has abused and dominated the family for decades, because they do not want their situation to become known. Until the shame settles clearly on the perpetrators, this will continue to be the case.

For many women, the threats of physical harm are real and serious. One woman reported that she knew when she was 'out of line' at a social gathering because her partner would offer to get her a cardigan. This was a warning that she would need it later to cover bruises. Another woman became alarmed when her partner illegally imported a Taser and kept it in the bedroom. He never used it, she did not know whether he would use it, but her fear was very real.

Some women report that there was physical violence earlier in their relationship, but 'he hasn't hit me for years'. He hasn't needed to, she knows what he is capable of and learned long ago to submit to his behaviour. She is subtly controlled by the fear that he will attack her again. This can apply even when there are only one or two physical assaults early in the relationship.

Pet abuse

The love of an animal can be a powerful tool for abusers to frighten and control victims. A form of abuse often used is to harm or threaten pets. People are often surprised to hear that there is a strong link between animal abuse and intimate partner violence. According to the American Humane Association, 71 per cent of pet-owning women entering women's shelters reported that their partner had injured, maimed, killed or threatened family pets.[3]

Cruelty to animals is often a warning sign of more abusive behaviour. One little boy told me his first memory of his father was that when he dirtied his pants, his daddy drowned his kitten. Threatening or torturing animals can demonstrate power and be a warning about what could happen to the victim if they displease them. Victims can be made to stay if they think their pet will be harmed if they leave. Remember, too, that people living in a refuge or transitional government housing are not allowed to have a pet.

Some domestic violence services have partnerships with animal shelters so that pets can be housed while women are seeking safety and a secure place to live. If you are afraid to leave a partner because your pet will be harmed, ask your domestic violence service for assistance.

Predicting danger

Women and children become attuned to the nuances of the perpetrator's behaviour. They become adept at gauging his mood to assess their safety, and adjust their behaviour. She also becomes astute at assessing the risk when the perpetrator changes the rules he is insisting she follows, usually without notice.

Research supporting a woman's ability to predict her partner's dangerousness is so well documented that the Common Risk Assessment Framework used by professionals across Victoria has the victim's assessment of her own safety as one of its three principles. Her assessment is weighed evenly with the other two assessment criteria and this approach is backed by international research.[4] This provides another argument against asking women, 'Why don't you just leave him?' They are making this assessment over and over again.

One of the key characteristics of violence against women is this climate of fear in the relationship. While some men are fearful of their partners, research suggests that few men who claim their partners have been violent to them also report that they fear them. These men may have been mistreated but they do not fear for their safety. This means it is far safer for them to leave relationships where they are abused or disrespected than women who live in fear of dangerous repercussions if they stand up to, or leave, abusive men. There is a much lower rate of stalking and violence against men once a woman leaves a relationship compared to that experienced by women after they leave men.[5]

Most women with abusive partners discover they will never get it right all the time and their partners will become dangerous again no matter how hard they try to please them. Even then, the combination of family responsibilities and fear may keep them there. Leaving him is the action most likely to anger him.

Most women who are murdered by their partners are planning to leave them or they have left. The most dangerous time is the first few weeks after leaving. Many women remain at risk for years after they leave.[6,7] I have spoken with women who are fearful their partner will 'come after them' to hurt them months and years after the relationship has ended.

Intimate partner violence has devastating effects

In Australia, on average, one woman is murdered by a current or former partner every week. This is a horrifying statistic. Many women suffer serious physical injuries due to assaults by their partners. Some women are permanently maimed by perpetrators, most commonly suffering head and facial injuries and damage to their hearing. Some women have been paralysed or suffer disabilities for the rest of their lives.

In addition, there are many thousands who mourn unborn children, having miscarried as a result of being assaulted while pregnant. This occurrence is commonly disclosed to domestic violence workers, but seems to be little known in the general community. Pregnancy is a well-documented risk factor for intimate partner violence,[8] and violence towards a woman often escalates during pregnancy. Never,

ever become pregnant to save a relationship or expect a pregnancy to improve the behaviour of a partner who uses any form of abuse.

There are other physical problems associated with the emotional toll of intimate partner violence including sleep disturbance, insomnia, intestinal problems, self-neglect and self-harm, chronic exhaustion and eating difficulties.

However, most lasting damage is not physical. Most physical injuries are lacerations, fractures and bruises. These heal, at least to some extent. If the damage were only physical, I would be out of business. Doctors and nurses would be handling the recovery process, not psychologists and counsellors.

By far the most common outcome of domestic violence is psychological trauma and distress such as long-term grief, post-traumatic stress, anxiety and depression.

The other common outcome is financial ruin. These, of course, affect each other with financial worry exacerbating psychological ill-health and yet making it harder to access help.

Living with intimate partner violence undermines your confidence day after day, and eats away at your soul. When I have asked women about the worst aspect, or the worst incident of abuse in their relationship, the reply almost invariably involves an experience of humiliation. Often it is not the worst instance of physical assault, it is when they have felt most shamed, worthless or degraded. It is usually when someone else notices how they are treated, often in public or in front of their children.

One way to understand what it might be like to live with a violent partner is to think about the victims as being in a kind of hostage situation. When we follow some of the terrible hostage situations in the news we can understand why those who survive might experience fears, nightmares, grief and anxiety. We can appreciate that they might have trouble getting back to work or feel nervous in certain places and situations.

Now, imagine the person taking you hostage is the person who had started out as your best friend. Then imagine that you have been a hostage for years, gradually being ground down to a shadow of your former competent self. Let us say that somehow you have found the courage to seek help and escape, but your tormentor has made it their business to track you down and hurt you in any way they can, perhaps by killing you. They may be the father of your children, so you have to see them and negotiate with them for years.

Survivors of domestic violence experience many types of psychological and emotional difficulties.

These are:

- Cognitive difficulties
- Learning difficulties
- Problems with decision making
- Problems with concentration

Emotional struggles

- Depression
- Pervasive anxiety
- Problems with anger
- Grief from a thousand losses of friends, opportunities, the self you used to like, the lifestyle you had or worked for
- Dealing with the loss of the future you wanted for yourself and for your children
- Erosion or fracturing of the mother-child bond due to a loss of confidence in your mothering abilities, or deliberate disparaging of you as a parent
- Post-traumatic stress symptoms (although the victim may still be living with ongoing trauma)
- Jumpiness and being always on the lookout for danger (known as hyper-vigilance)
- Flashbacks
- Nightmares
- Sleeplessness, exhaustion
- Emotional numbing, losing interest in how you feel about anything

Problems with your social life

- Impaired ability to form or maintain friendships
- Social isolation, real or self-imposed because of fear
- Sense of dislocation from others
- Distrust of strangers (and new friends)
- Anxiety about meeting new people

Existential damage — the soul-destroying stuff

- Loss of a sense of personal autonomy, or control over your own life
- Loss of the ability to trust others, and to trust the world, such as losing a sense of safety
- Self-loathing
- Hopelessness
- Guilt and shame
- An overwhelming sense of betrayal

I am frequently in awe of women who come for help after experiencing domestic violence. I have witnessed courage and heroism that inspires and astonishes me.

The positive end to this terrible list of difficulties is that women and children do recover. Never assume that a woman's distressed state as she escapes an abusive relationship is a permanent one. It is amazing how well women recover when they are no longer being routinely belittled, abused, undermined and assaulted.

CHAPTER FIVE
WHY DOES HE DO IT?

One question that is frequently asked is, 'Why does he do that?' which is also the name of an excellent book on the subject by Lundy Bancroft.[1] One way to look at domestic violence is to look at the underlying motivation of the perpetrator. This has its drawbacks as different motivations can drive any type of behaviour, but it allows us to connect the use of violence and abuse to the person choosing to behave in these ways.

There are certainly common characteristics among people who like to exert power and control over their partners. Here are some types of behaviour that occur in the context of domestic violence. They are grouped according to what they reveal about someone who behaves this way.

Being self-centred

- Selfishness, vanity and a pre-occupation with their own affairs and desires
- Not caring about a partner's feelings or trying to talk them out of the way they feel
- Always talking about themselves, and not showing an interest in what their partner is doing or cares about
- Spending money on what they want and complaining about what their partner wants

An outrageous sense of entitlement

- A belief that their needs and wants come first, their wishes deserve to be prioritised, and their beliefs are more valid than those of others
- Assuming that their opinions are the only ones that count
- Expecting to be waited on

- Not doing their share of chores
- Constantly putting off agreed tasks
- Trying to make decisions for their partner that they would normally make for themselves
- Wanting things 'on demand', including in the bedroom
- Sulking or getting angry if they do not get their way

A refusal to take responsibility

- Not taking responsibility for their mistakes and shortcomings
- Blaming their partner for whatever goes wrong
- Blaming others when it is they who are in the wrong
- Never apologising
- Pseudo-apologising, such as saying they are 'sorry you are upset', but not for what they have done
- Giving long explanations and excuses when they stuff up
- Not pulling their weight and not paying their share of expenses
- Borrowing money and not paying it back
- Burdening their partner with financial commitments that they have not agreed to

A lack of respect

- Showing disrespect or contempt for your partner
- Failing to respect their privacy, such as laughing when asked to knock before barging into the bathroom
- Listening to their partner's phone calls, checking their messages or reading their emails without permission
- Criticising or making fun of their partner so the partner feels diminished
- Ridiculing their partner in front of others
- Denying there is a problem when their partner voices their concerns
- Ridiculing or insulting their partner's looks or body

- Demanding or coercing their partner to lose or gain weight, or making them exercise or have surgery to change their appearance
- Treating their partner like a child

A desire to dominate

- Being willing to intimidate to get their own way, and to make threats
- Using emotional blackmail to get their own way; for example, making their partner afraid to take a break from the relationship
- Threatening to hurt their partner
- Threatening to hurt their partner's friends or family
- Threatening to hurt a partner's pet
- Threatening to hurt themselves if their partner leaves them
- Damaging something in anger or to show their potential for violence, such as punching a wall
- Intimidating their partner, such as standing over them

Jealousy and suspicion

- A belief that their partner belongs to them and/or that their partner must not have friendships of which they do not approve, usually coupled with frequent suspicion about their partner's friendships and social contacts
- Constantly accusing their partner of flirting
- Accusing their partner of being unfaithful when they are not
- Claiming that their partner dresses deliberately to attract other men/women
- Objecting if their partner wants to spend time with friends or family
- Checking up on their partner all the time
- Calling their partner often when they are out, constantly wanting to know where they are, what they are doing, who they are with, what time they will be home

Physical, sexual and emotional abuse

This list is sadly endless …

- Yelling at their partner, calling them names
- Destroying or damaging their things
- Sadism, such as laughing when their partner or others are hurt
- Demanding sex or coercing their partner to have sex when they do not want to
- Trying to get their partner to do things sexually that make them feel uncomfortable or hurt them
- Telling jokes about their partner or deliberately embarrassing them
- Scaring their partner deliberately, such as driving dangerously to scare their partner
- Hitting, slapping, punching and any form of physical assault
- Shoving or throwing their partner against a wall or onto a bed
- Spitting at, pinching a partner or pulling their hair
- Holding them down
- Choking them
- Forcing them to take drugs when they don't want to
- Pressuring them to get pregnant, or tampering with their birth control method
- Harming their pets
- Questioning their reality, known as 'gas-lighting'[2]

Controlling behaviour

- Controlling and punishing their partner
- Telling their partner what they can or cannot do, say, think, wear, cook, buy, etc.
- Not allowing their partner access to their own money or to joint family money
- Not allowing their partner to leave the house, holding them hostage in any way or for any length of time

- Insisting their partner follow their decisions or orders
- Insisting their partner do things their way
- Punishing their partner for doing, or not doing, something according to their rules
- Stopping their partner doing what they want to do for themselves or their children
- Giving their partner a curfew

Acting as if they own you

- Visiting or waiting near places their partners frequent, such as their workplace or their parent's home, to check up on them
- Following or watching their partner, with or without their knowledge
- Keeping electronic track of their partner's movements, such as via the GPS in a car or phone
- Unwanted letters, gifts, emails or phone calls, including unwanted love letters
- Prank calls and hang-ups
- Using tracking devices to stalk a partner or former partner

Double standards

- Shouting at their partner, but if she shouts, labelling her as 'hysterical'
- Flirting (or having affairs) but not allowing their partner to talk to other men
- Demanding their partner account for every expense, but not sharing how they spend money
- Insisting on knowing where their partner is at all times, but not telling them where they go or what they are doing
- Pointing out their partner's faults but denying they have any

Sexual abuse in a relationship

One of the hidden but common horrors of intimate partner violence is sexual abuse. There is a difference between being sexually assaulted by a stranger and being sexually assaulted by a partner or former partner. Most sexual assaults by strangers are a single incident, and this means you are unlikely to blame yourself or to doubt that what has happened was a sexual assault.

If the person who rapes you is someone whom you have loved, and perhaps still love, this is not only a sexual assault, it is a massive betrayal of trust. This person, whom you have trusted not only with your dreams and secrets but also with your body, has become your rapist which is psychologically shocking, confusing and humiliating.

When a woman has been sexually assaulted in a relationship, it is likely to keep recurring. This can really mess with her mind because she can wonder if she is partly responsible or she questions her right to say 'no' to sex, or questions whether she is somehow to blame.

I remember one woman who would not wear makeup or attractive clothing at home, in case it led to her being sexually assaulted. Our discussion revealed just how much she tortured herself about not wanting a sexual relationship with a man who verbally and emotionally abused her dozens of times a day, but expected sex every evening.

Some sexual violence in the context of intimate partner violence involves physical violence, and the use of weapons and restraints. This type of abuse is extremely humiliating. There are abusers who sexually assault their partners after physically attacking them, and maintain that this is part of the victim demonstrating forgiveness.

Often, though, extreme physical violence is not used and sexual assault occurs by the use of coercion of some sort. As expected, the partner-rapist is used to getting his own way and the victim is finely attuned to reducing harm to herself. She may want to get it over with, or not wake the children, or may see her wishes as not as important or valid. The concept of conjugal rights is one I have often heard from victims of sexual coercion and assault within marriages.

Many partner rapists continue to assault or coerce their partners after the relationship has ended, even when the women have moved out. Many women have spoken about former partners who keep visiting and demanding sex after they have moved out. They also speak about giving in to these demands because they are frightened to refuse them.

They are often judged badly for this.

Like much restriction and control over women's autonomy, it is not long ago that sexual consent was seen as almost irrelevant in marriage. In the USA, it was not until 1993 that spousal rape became a crime in all 50 states.[3]

In Australia, the states took a similar time-span to come on board (1976-1989) and for some years it did not equate marital with non-marital rape. In the case of marital rape, violence or aggravating circumstances had to be present if the victim was married to the aggressor.[4]

Sex is one of our most beautiful, personal and intimate experiences. As such, it should only occur in the context of full and free consent, every single time.

Sexual abuse is not often disclosed by survivors due to the high level of shame and humiliation involved with this type of abuse. Some women see counsellors for months but never reveal their experiences of sexual abuse.

There is absolute certainty that someone who won't take 'NO' for an answer in the living room, will definitely not take 'NO' for an answer in the bedroom.

CHAPTER SIX

PHYSICAL v PSYCHOLOGICAL ABUSE

Conversations in the public arena about intimate partner violence have changed in the last decade. We are moving from a concept of domestic violence as being about physical violence to a broader understanding of the range of behaviours that blight victims' lives. Legal definitions of domestic violence have broadened to include many aspects of abuse, including exposing children to domestic violence as witnesses. I am frequently asked: What is worse, physical abuse or psychological abuse?

All violence, including physical abuse, involves emotional or psychological abuse. You simply cannot be hit without it affecting you emotionally. Whether you are being physically attacked as part of that abuse or not, you are being emotionally attacked. There is no type of abuse that does not affect the victim emotionally. Therefore, the question of what is worse, physical or psychological abuse, is irrelevant for two reasons. The first is because you cannot have physical abuse without psychological abuse, the second is because both can cause long lasting and sometimes irreparable harm.

Sonya and Greg

Greg is a lawyer. Originally he was a policeman, but left the force when he obtained a scholarship to study law. Sonya is a nurse, a stunning blonde whose father is a retired judge from a well-off family. They had the kind of courtship and wedding you see in Hollywood movies — dates at the best restaurants, skiing holidays in winter and seeing in the New Year from her uncle's yacht on Sydney Harbour. The wedding was big and beautiful and the honeymoon was a month in Paris and London. Both have successful careers and they have three beautiful, clever children.

Sonya did not identify herself as being a victim of domestic violence; she had sought help for anxiety and insomnia, and wondered whether she was depressed. Among other things, I asked her about her home life and any stresses she was dealing with.

Sonya told me a very familiar tale. She wondered if there was something wrong with her, and could I please tell her what, because Greg was so nice to everyone else and so unpleasant to her. He would belittle her cooking, her body, her choice of clothes and the way she read stories to the children. He disapproved of her friends and interests, ridiculed the church group she had joined, and would threaten her or sulk if he did not get his own way. Her life revolved around not upsetting him. Recently, Sonya had reluctantly declined an invitation to take the children to spend Easter in New York with her parents at their expense, because Greg had said the 'whole idea was ridiculous' and too disruptive for the children.

Sonya was clearly embarrassed to be seeing me, vacillating between shame and despair as she told her story. She said she had so much to be grateful for with her lifestyle, her children were all at private schools and Greg was 'a good provider'.

She said she thought of Greg as 'Mr Perfect' and just wasn't sure she was a 'good wife'. She didn't want to have sex as often as he did (which was at least daily), she 'forgot things' (she had recently forgotten to renew his car registration) and she seemed to be getting worse. She found she was tired all the time and becoming more miserable at the thought that she could never please him.

What was wrong with Sonya, and could I help her? Was Sonya depressed, or just oppressed?

The effects of psychological abuse

One of the important elements of intimate partner violence is fear. Why is fear so important? The main reason is that the threat of harm is real and significant, especially so if the person has acted out threats in the past, even only once.

This means that a person becomes jumpy and super-alert, what psychologists call 'hyper-vigilant' where they are always looking over their shoulder or gauging their immediate safety. This takes a lot of time and energy, and the classic image of a worn down woman who suffers lots of violence at home indeed occurs — people can end up looking and feeling wasted and ill. It's just that the abuse does not have to be physical for this to happen.

Emotional or psychological abuse can be hard to recognise and to comprehend. It threatens the way people think and feel about themselves and the world. It can lead to long-term anxiety and tension, and can seriously undermine a person's ability to function in the world. Sustained psychological abuse can be like programming or even brainwashing. Sometimes the perpetrator's view of their partner replaces the partner's own beliefs about herself, and the victim ends up quite debilitated. It can be life-threatening, if someone becomes suicidally depressed or starts to rely on drugs or alcohol to self-medicate their emotional distress. It often takes much longer to heal than physical wounds.

Raelene and Robert

Raelene was a shy, hard-working library assistant. She loved ballet and was a talented watercolour artist in her spare time. Rob always insisted on being in charge and in the early days some of this suited Raelene because she trusted him. He managed their money, chose with whom they would socialise and where they would holiday. Only once, early in the relationship, had she tried to make a major decision, wanting to apply for a more senior position in another library. Rob had told her in no uncertain terms what a stupid idea that was, and that she had no chance of being able to keep on top of everything at home if she moved to a more demanding job.

Over the 18 years they spent together Raelene did most of the parenting of their two children and most of the domestic chores. This was life, as Raelene knew it. In her mind, she and Rob drifted apart and eventually had little to talk about and no interests in common. He had once agreed to attend a local art show where some of her work had been included in an exhibition. He poured scorn on her work, called her a 'rank amateur' and her work an 'embarrassment'. She left the hall in tears and never forgot the humiliation of that evening, nor did she paint again until long after their marriage ended.

Raelene's sister told her once that she had become a 'mouse' and should get out more and 'make some friends'. Raelene explained that Rob liked everything to be a certain way, and that he got 'frustrated' if dinner was not on time or the children left their things in the living area. She did not explain to her sister that Rob would say vile things to her, often called her a 'moron' even in front of the children, and that he sometimes refused to speak to her at all for weeks. Raelene knew she was unhappy, but did not think of herself as being abused. The marriage ended when Rob told Raelene one evening, in three sentences, that he had not loved her for years and was leaving to live with a woman he had been seeing for over a year.

Raelene went into shock. She was, by this time, anxious, jumpy and timid, and sometimes felt panicky for no apparent reason. She had trouble making the most basic decisions and believed that she could do nothing right. She felt a complete failure, which is exactly how Rob had treated her for as long as she could remember. It took years of regular support before she regained the self-esteem that had been stripped from her by constant psychological abuse. Perhaps Rob was well named.

This scenario demonstrates some of the reasons that psychological or emotional abuse is so destructive. First, it was constantly happening, it became part of the fabric of Raelene's life. Secondly, Raelene believed she had almost brought it on herself, she felt so undeserving and useless that she blamed herself for ruining the marriage.

If someone hits you or screams at you it is easier to see that they are at least part of the problem. If you are constantly told you are fat, ugly, stupid or worthless and that everyone thinks so, you are more likely to believe that you are the problem.

This is especially so if you have little or no reality check; in other words, there is no-one to counter that view because you have become isolated from others who know you better. This type of abuse is intensely personal, and it is an attack on your sense of yourself, your self-worth. Long after the scars of physical abuse have healed, you may still be battling to believe in yourself.

Caleb and Tessa

Tessa and Caleb met online and moved in together after a few months. Caleb seemed to have particular ways of doing things, he had to have his car parked closest to the flat in a certain spot, even if Tessa came home first. He liked a clean towel every time he washed and he even showed her a 'better' way to peg out her washing. He wanted to accompany her on shopping trips, even for clothes and food, always miffed if she did not like his suggestions for her purchases.

When she visited her family while he was at work he called her once or twice an hour to see if she was still there and when she was leaving. He hated her talking to other men at social gatherings, and even accused her of 'having the hots' for his brother.

Caleb always had a better way of doing things; he belittled her opinions, her friends, her choices and her achievements. He did not hit her, but he did make her life a misery. He checked her email and phone messages and social media accounts, sometimes responding, pretending to be her.

Tessa was a strong woman, a paramedic team leader, but she was afraid of Caleb becoming upset with her. She became more anxious and depressed over time, and was referred by her doctor for counselling. Later, she said that looking back she couldn't work out how it happened, that she became so intimidated by Caleb. She told me her life was no longer her own.

After she left, Caleb stalked Tessa for months. She came home to find he had re-pegged her washing on the clothesline in his own special style, and would leave notes on her car, just so she knew that he knew where she was and what she was doing. He had downloaded spyware that allowed him to read her emails and texts, though she did not find this out until nearly a year after she left him. It took an Intervention Order and the threat of a conviction for breaches of that order to get him to stop.

Try to imagine how this affected Tessa both within, and after, she left the relationship. She had never been physically injured or even physically threatened. In the beginning she resented being told what to buy or what to do, but then accepted his 'foibles' for the sake of peace. She lost faith in her own ability to make decisions for herself, and would check with him about how to do things she had been doing for herself without a hitch before they met. She suffered extreme anxiety when she was being stalked. It seemed to her that he knew where she was and what she was doing all the time. She never knew when he might go to her new flat while she was out or if he would turn up when she was home.

She tried taking practical precautions, even paying for parking in a nearby carpark at night so that he would not leave notes on her car. She hated having to wonder what he was doing or planning for her. She dried her washing inside and eventually traded in her car hoping he would not know what her new car looked like —this worked for three days!

Then, just as she was regaining her psychological strength and felt strong again, she discovered accidentally that he had put spyware on her computer and had been privy to her emails for a whole year, including her emails to her friends, her family and her lawyer. She was once again very depressed, describing herself at this point as 'trapped forever' by his toxicity. Remember what I said about victims of domestic violence feeling like hostages? This is exactly how Tessa felt.

A word about jealousy

One very common form of psychological abuse is when a partner is repeatedly accused of having an affair or of wanting to have an affair or flirting, when none of this is the case.

This is such a common accusation that counsellors who work with survivors are never surprised to hear it.

It has been suggested that partners who keep making such accusations might be secretly worried or guilty about their own desire to be unfaithful, a theory that Freud would be proud of. As I do not normally meet the partners of the women who report this, and I am not a private detective, I cannot test that out.

Many of the women subject to such suspicion are too afraid to even look at another man. Clearly, such accusations are just another manifestation of controlling behaviour.

Often, the accuser then wants to control what the partner wears, who they talk to, where they go, what they do socially. They want to listen to their phone calls, check their social media and so on — it is jealousy in a dangerous form and many women who end up being stalked have experienced these types of accusations.

While exclusivity is expected in most long-term relationships it does not mean ownership, and it does not justify such controlling behaviour. The accusations continue, and sometimes escalate, when a woman has made it clear that the relationship is over. This behaviour implies a belief that the victim belongs to their partner, and the accusations rarely go away even if the woman can prove they are baseless.

I am shocked, at times, about how early some men move into this type of jealousy; working in schools has taught me how common such accusations are in very early dating relationships.

If a man has convinced himself that his partner is cheating or flirting or wants to chase someone else, there is usually little she can say to convince him. If his motivation is to stay in control of her and his accusations are baseless and just feeding this motivation, he will be unlikely to change his thinking. I have seen plenty of women who have changed their clothes and their friends, or denied themselves social activities, so that their partner is not upset by their behaviour. Does this help? If it does, it's very temporary. Usually, it does not help at all.

I guess for some men clear evidence would mitigate that particular accusation, but I predict it would be replaced by another accusation or some other controlling behaviour.

Women trying to walk on eggshells do learn things to say or do in their particular relationships and it might stave off some immediate danger, but it does not change the dynamic in the relationship. In fact, it confirms who is in charge, and it's not her.

Are women more abusive emotionally?

Often when I speak publicly about domestic violence, I am asked to remember that 'women can be just as abusive emotionally'. Some people have assured me that women are 'as bad as men are' or are 'much more able to destroy a man verbally'.

I have spoken to men who talk about being abused by their partners, and they usually talk about being criticised or made to feel they are 'less than a man'. Examples would be: 'You're pathetic, my last boyfriend was much better in bed than you'll ever be.' Or, 'You're too stupid to earn decent money.' Their partners seem to be targeting their fear of being inadequate — as a lover, a provider or as a father.

Consistent abuse like this certainly does undermine a person's self-worth and causes long-term emotional pain. The aim is to make a man feel shamed and miserable, but this does not mean he is afraid.

When I talk to women about verbal and emotional abuse, something different is often going on. Their partners threaten to hurt them, to isolate them from their friends, to harm their pets or harm their children.

The aim is to dominate and intimidate, in other words to create fear. This is more dangerous, both because it contains threats of physical danger and because being controlled through fear by someone much more powerful than oneself is more psychologically damaging than being ridiculed and shamed. As we discussed earlier, fear is the major factor in controlling behaviour.

CHAPTER SEVEN

THINKING ABOUT THE CHILDREN

It has been estimated that somewhere between 750,000 and more than one million Australian children are living with violence.[1]

Apart from those who come to physical harm, this causes a wide range of difficulties for those children. A large proportion of the women seeking help with abuse at home are mothers of dependent children. The impact on children is often the primary consideration for those mothers.

If someone is abusing a mother then they are abusing her child, too. They undermine a child's sense of safety in the world and their trust of adults in general, and negatively affect their emotional and educational development.

There are myriad ways to undermine a partner's parenting. Some of them, commonly heard by people working with domestic violence victims, include:

- Humiliating a mother in front of her children
- Speaking badly about a mother to her children or in front of her children
- Sabotaging her parenting, such as telling the children not to listen to her
- Interfering with the bond between a woman and her child, such as not allowing her to breastfeed/bottle feed
- Not allowing a mother to attend to, or comfort, her child
- Demeaning or insulting her parenting
- Not following up agreed parenting decisions
- Assaulting her verbally, physically or sexually

Most assaults on parents are witnessed by children, even if the parents think this is not the case. Children are affected equally as much as if they had been assaulted themselves.[2] One seven-year-old was referred with recurrent nightmares, and described vividly the monsters who were fighting in his house when he went to sleep. He was afraid they would attack him in the night. Eventually his mother confided that she and her husband had many 'terrible fights', but that her son knew nothing about these fights because they only happened when he was asleep.

In another family, with two young daughters, the mother would try to ensure the children were asleep before her husband came home drunk. The girls would pretend to be asleep, but try hard to stay awake so they could be there to protect their mother. All three were pretending in some fashion most of the time, and the father was simply getting away with his violence.

Children are often also burdened with the responsibility of keeping their family's terrible secrets, and sometimes of looking after their mother after an assault. Many children develop problem behaviours such as angry outbursts, clinginess, nailbiting or nervousness, or conditions such as bed-wetting or anxiety.

Children often feel torn in terms of who to believe and who to trust when there is violence. Perhaps one parent teaches them not to believe or respect the other, or a parent who is abusive may appear to be strong and in charge.

There is the huge issue of anticipated loss with young children, particularly when they live in fear of losing a parent through violence.

They may feel terribly guilty about not being able to keep the abusing parent happy, or not behaving well enough or not thinking or feeling the 'right' way.

Then there are the social implications for children who cannot take friends home because their parent's violence is too unpredictable, and they may learn to lie about how things are at home. When parents separate and there has been violence, they can experience fear about threats or continued harassment, and wonder what will happen to both parents. Above all, they may feel they are not normal and experience a great sense of shame about not having a 'normal' family.

Some of the saddest research has studied small infants who live with violence, and the effects on babies can be clearly seen in the damage done to their relationship with their mothers. Their emotional and cognitive development is also affected.

Domestic violence is an assault on the mother-child bond, right from the start, and all throughout childhood.[3]

There are many good resources for helping children, but the biggest help is for the violence to stop, and that needs to be paramount. While the community expects the non-abusive parent to protect the child, they may not always be able to do so. In such cases, the community needs to take a role by preventing the abusive parent from harming the child and their protective parent. This is why child protection services need a thorough understanding of the dynamics of intimate partner abuse.

If you know a child in this situation you might be the only advocate, apart from the protective parent, that child has. Try not to judge the adult victim, they are no doubt doing the very best they can.

One unfortunate side-effect of recognising that witnessing domestic violence is bad for a child and including it in the definition of family violence is that the blame can move to the mother for failing to protect the child from abuse and violence. My work has often involved children whose situation has been reported to child protection services. These services often end up working primarily with a non-abusive mother because the person using violence, whose behaviour has been causing concern, is uncooperative. He won't attend meetings or won't go for his drug tests, assessments or counselling sessions.

Too often, in an effort to protect the children, the onus falls on the mother to stop the violence affecting the child. Many times I have seen a team of counsellors, social workers and lawyers working hard with the mother to try to stop the violence from occurring, while the abusive father or step-father cannot even be made to attend a meeting.

Reading the book by Rosie Batty[4] gives us a salutary example of the system trying but failing to protect a child because the person who is being violent just keeps on being abusive and is not held to account. If we want someone to stop abusing a child, we need to deal with the perpetrator, and the community is often still very poor at doing that.

Why we have to get it right for the children

The way we deal with children is the key to the future.

If we are to provide a secure home for children, we have to reduce domestic violence

Domestic and family violence is the number one reason why people present to specialist homelessness services, with 55 per cent of female clients citing this reason.[5]

If we are to reduce the incidence of mental illness, we have to reduce domestic violence

Domestic violence is a factor in up to 25 per cent of female suicide attempts. Female victims of domestic violence have eight times the risk for suicide compared with the general population. And 50 per cent of female victims of domestic violence who attempt suicide undertake subsequent attempts.[6]

Living with violence can have long-term effects on a child's future mental health. In my experience many clients presenting to counselling services with concerns about their mental health report growing up with domestic violence.

If we are to reduce drug and alcohol abuse, we have to reduce domestic violence

According to one NSW report, about 60 per cent of women undertaking substance abuse treatments are current domestic violence victims.[7]

Young people who have lived with violence are at risk of developing problems with alcohol and drug use. Evidence from the USA suggests that between 41 and 80 per cent of women in alcohol and drug treatment programs have experienced family violence.[8] Boys who have grown up with violence are also at increased risk of substance abuse.[9]

If we are to reduce both the male and female prison population, we have to reduce domestic violence

A high proportion of both male and female prison inmates have grown up with violence at home, and one study found that a third have been in out-of-home care as children.[10]

Sisters Inside, an independent community organisation that advocates for women's rights, observed that many women in prison are survivors of domestic violence. It found 98 per cent of women in prison have experienced physical violence.

A whopping 90 per cent of incarcerated women are survivors of sexual abuse. Horrific stories of domestic violence form the backgrounds to many of the more serious crimes committed by women.[11]

If we are to improve academic outcomes for the most disadvantaged children, we have to reduce domestic violence

An Australian Institute of Family Studies report revealed that living with family violence makes it hard for children to learn. It found '... 67 per cent of children exposed to domestic and family violence were at risk of a range of developmental and adjustment problems and fared worse than other children in terms of academic success, cognitive ability, mental health and wellbeing ... children's exposure to domestic and family violence was associated with a range of cognitive and behavioural problems and poorer academic outcomes.'[12]

> The bottom line is this: The more children who grow up free from violence and with positive views about gender equality and relationships, the less domestic violence there will be in the future.

CHAPTER EIGHT

WHY DOES SHE STAY?

This is the question the community should just stop asking!

In western cultures, there were few options for women being abused at home until the mid-20th century when the women's liberation movement led to more open discussions about domestic abuse. The first women's shelters opened in the 1960s. In 2014, VicHealth released the results of a national survey of community attitudes. More than half of the respondents agreed with the statement: 'Most women could leave a violent relationship if they wanted to.'[1]

And 78 per cent agreed with, 'It's hard to understand why women stay.'

Most people who try to imagine what they would do if they were living with domestic violence think they would leave if not after the first time there was violence, then certainly after the second. The paradox is that they are often right. Victims would also leave if they could, so why don't they?

For a start, leaving is usually a process, not a single action. For most women there are practical and financial things to consider when leaving, as well as their safety once they make the decision.

There are often strong reasons to stay as well as to go, and it can be very confusing. No wonder many women leave a number of times before finally leaving for the last time.

As discussed earlier, they are often torn between their own needs and what they see as their responsibilities and obligations to their families or to the perpetrator.

In the beginning, the abuse is often seen by the woman as an aberration, out of character for the person they love.

There is, of course, the threat of physical harm, but there are other very significant threats such as having no money or resources, having to leave home and having nowhere to go, the censure or possible cutting off from family members or their own networks, and having to deal with the often terrible distress of their children.

They fear for their future in a hundred ways.

Women may stay because their partner has threatened to kill himself. This can lay an enormous amount of guilt on the woman, especially if this could mean their children would grow up without their father.

She may believe that his or her relatives, or their children, would blame her for his death. 'If only she hadn't left him.'

'Couldn't she have tried to work it out, especially for the children?'

Such threats also have a very sinister side. A person who is prepared to kill themselves has very little to lose. Think about those men who kill themselves after killing their partners or children. A threat that he will kill himself is bad enough, but with it comes a raft of other implied threats.

A woman may stay because she hopes that he will become again the man she first knew and loved. They have usually invested an enormous amount into the relationship. They may have children, which can be both a reason to go and a reason to stay. Perpetrators often voice some remorse and make wonderful promises that victims want to believe. Perhaps he will change, perhaps he will go to that counsellor or men's group.

Women may stay because they think they have to help their partner learn to behave like a loving human being. Often the couple's family, friends or pastor join in this chorus. One woman I know was told, 'You married for better or worse, and he can't manage without you.' Some men feed this belief by telling their partners that they are the only ones who can help them.

Some women feel partly responsible, perhaps they should be better housekeepers or mothers. Isn't he always telling them better ways to do things? She may do a bit too much drinking or spending, and feel responsible for his use of violence towards her. I have met women who believe their depression is driving their partners to be violent, rather than his violence is a factor in their depression.

Some men threaten to harm or kill their partner if the violence is reported to anyone, and some carry out this threat.

Some women stay because the emotional abuse has been so thorough and so relentless that they no longer believe they can manage on their own. Their positive view of themselves, if they had one, has been replaced by his negative view of them and they just feel hopeless.

Many women feel trapped, because they are.

Many perpetrators are skilled at closing down their partner's external support network of friends and family. When the woman is ready to leave, there may be no one to go to for help and no one to offer support. Many women are unaware of the support services provided by community agencies, or have been turned away, or think that these options are for other women, worse off than they are.

Many women are dependent on their partners for financial support, and even if they earn a living they have not been allowed to manage their finances. This economic dependence can cripple any chance to escape and rebuild their lives.

Many women believe the lies they are told by their partner:

> *'You'll never make it on your own.'*
>
> *'No-one will ever believe you.'*
>
> *'The children will hate you for it.'*

Some women stay for the children, believing it is better to take the abuse than for their children to live without their father.

Many men threaten that the woman will not see her children, or that she will be reported for child abuse, if she leaves.

Many women are committed to marriage, or have religious or cultural reasons that make leaving a marriage an even bigger nightmare than otherwise.

Many women stay because they have nowhere to go. It's as simple as that.

Overall, the most common reason to stay is fear, and there is much to be fearful about. They may be living with real threats to themselves, their children or their families, and these are not to be underestimated.

A few years ago someone started a Twitterfeed called #WhyIStayed. The women responding to this feed are more eloquent than I could ever be.

> *He convinced me it was my fault and that it was something wrong with me.*

I thought the pushing and shoving was normal. My mother always convinced me to go back.

He was a veteran, and his family didn't believe me, making me look crazy.

I thought that if I tried harder, he'd change. I was terrified of being a single mom.

I knew no one else would want me. I was lucky that he chose me.

I finally left because he almost killed me. Humiliation, shame, recrimination.

I thought all men were the same. Because the abuse becomes your norm.

Because I thought you'd find a way to kill me if I left.

Because you had me brainwashed into believing your word was god.

I thought it was 'love'.

I thought it was my fault and I deserved it.

I tried to leave the house once and he blocked me. He slept in front of the door that entire night.

Why does she keep going back?

This question is sometimes asked by friends and relatives of women who have helped and supported her to leave a relationship, and then become frustrated when she returns.

The answer to this question is always complex, and these are just examples of the many reasons that lead to women returning to men who have abused them.

- The emotions that led to their decision to leave such as fear, anger or resentment, may have subsided.
- They may believe his commitment to end the abuse or seek help.
- They may feel anxious, lonely or even guilty, and this is often reinforced by their partner.

- They may be pressured by family, friends or members of their community.
- They may fear poverty or the struggle to maintain their lifestyle.
- They may think it would be better for the children.
- The process of seeking help may be so daunting that they do not think a different life is possible.
- They may be too frightened not to give in to the demands of their partner.
- They may be afraid of losing contact with, or custody of, their children.
- They may believe his view that they cannot manage on their own.
- They may be too afraid of his threats not to return.
- They may be intimidated by the involvement of police or the legal system.
- They may not have been able to access sufficient support to help them stay safe.
- The post-separation abuse may be harder to deal with than the abuse before they left.
- They may believe the partner's promises to change.

In other words, it can seem that there are just as many good reasons to return as to leave. Some women feel less in control when they are not with their partner, simply because they no longer know what he is up to or when he may appear to attack them. They feel that if they are with him, they can keep track of his behaviour and therefore monitor their own safety.

CHAPTER NINE
HEARING AND HELPING

If I know a victim, what should I do?

I am hoping that some readers have picked up this book because they want to help someone they know and are worried about.

Helping in such circumstances is both very simple and very complex. There are basic guidelines but there is also a need to carefully consider the individual complexity of every situation. If you suspect someone you know is suffering at home, you will need to be diplomatic and patient. If you are worried about bringing up the topic, try to ask a general question like 'How are things at home?' Or say something generally supportive such as, 'Let me know if you need help with the family.' You might be able to show support without saying anything, such as asking their child for a play date with yours, or dropping off a cake or casserole. Include women you are worried about in invitations, and do not take it personally if they are ignored or refused.

Your kindness will be remembered, and will be an antidote to the emotional impact of living with abuse. One client told me she eventually went to a neighbour for help because that neighbour kindly brought over fruit mince pies for her family every Christmas.

Calling the police

If you believe someone's safety is at immediate risk then call 000. Do not call your partner, their mother or the local police station.

Treat the abuse as a crime and call 000. Insist on a response if you have to, but usually the police are ready and willing to dispatch the nearest police car. Call 000 if you think there is danger, or if the victim thinks they or others are in danger. Be someone who acts rather than ignores the distress of another — be an up stander — not just a bystander.

Do not put yourself at risk but if you can, try to get yourself and the victim to safety. If all you can say is the address and leave the call open, then do that. There is a great YouTube clip following the story of a call made in America to 911 where the woman pretended to be ordering a pizza in order to get help.[1]

Sometimes, even during an assault, victims are too afraid to call police and you might need to make the decision. Sometimes helpful bystanders think they can calm the perpetrator down, but if someone is asking for help or seems pursued or distressed call the police rather than put yourself at risk.

Another reason to call the police in such a situation is that the perpetrator may be able to terrify the victim and yet be completely calm and reasonable with you. Once you have left the scene, the violence will resume.

I have lost count of how many women have told me about situations where family, neighbours or police have intervened, been reassured by the perpetrator, and the violence starts again as soon as the people who could potentially help them have gone. This leaves the victim in a potentially more dangerous situation, and the perpetrator with an experience of greater power. He may also be enraged by the intervention and take his anger out on the victim with increased violence.

Police codes of practice around Australia vary but most police procedures will ensure the couple is interviewed separately, which gives the victim the chance to decide whether they wish to have the perpetrator or themselves go to a different place.

No matter how reasonable the perpetrator may appear when a third party intervenes, it is unlikely he will allow a bystander to speak privately to his abused partner, and if you manage to do this it may actually increase her risk after you leave the scene.

Police can insist that the victim is allowed to speak to them separately.

What is helpful?
The first need for anyone being abused, intimidated or bullied is safety. The first step to safety is a safe place to talk about it; a place where they

will be believed and supported and not judged, and not have to listen to a lot of well-meaning advice.

It is OK to ask questions once you have heard what they have to say.

- Listen well, and believe what you hear. It takes a lot of courage to talk about domestic violence and it carries a lot of shame.

- Let them know you have heard and believed them.

- You might thank them for trusting you with such personal information.

- Respect their confidentiality. Ask them who knows and if you think others should be told, ask whether this would be supportive.

- Tell them they are not to blame for the violence and abuse. If you have read this far, you will know that violence is a choice and the person making that choice is responsible for the violence. You can explain this to victims who feel responsible.

- See if they need help getting any information that will assist them. Perhaps you can get pamphlets for them, seek out services, or go on the Internet with them. The important thing is that they are part of this process and you are not taking over. Follow the woman's requests or advice on the provision of any supportive material or service documentation (even something as innocent seeming as a welfare payment application form or referral to a community health centre) as it may increase her risk if the perpetrator finds it.

- Try to suspend your own advice and judgement and just stand in their shoes. Then remember that even in their shoes, you might want to go in a different direction or at a different pace.

- Be patient, really patient. No matter what you think is best, they need to be in charge of their lives. This is exactly what has been taken away from them. If someone has been living with a partner who controls them, orders them around and makes decisions for them regardless of their wishes then it is no help if you start doing that as well. Worse still, the woman you are concerned about may withdraw from you as well for fear of angering or disappointing you.

- Ask them what would be helpful for them at this point in time, as this puts them in charge of the process.

- Above all, realise that although you are seeing this person in a very vulnerable state, do not assume they are not resourceful or strong.

- Leave them feeling supported and hopeful, even if that hope is only due to your support. Being believed without being judged is more powerful than you can imagine.

What is not helpful?

- Don't regale them with your own relationship experiences, save that until later. Much later. If ever. It is likely that for her it is neither relevant nor helpful.

- Don't assume that what worked for you, or what you think would work for you, will necessarily work for them.

- Don't ask why he does that. If you need help with this one, read this book again.

- Don't move into rescue mode, it will lead to you making decisions for them. This can be disempowering and disrespectful. If she has survived this far she is tougher and more resilient than you might think.

- Don't, please don't, sympathise with, excuse or try to analyse the perpetrator. For a start, you will probably get it wrong, and most importantly, it doesn't matter.

- The person needs and deserves to be safe from abuse. Her needs and feelings are paramount and she has had to subjugate these for long enough. Helping time is her time. Keep your focus on her.

- Equally, don't denigrate or malign the perpetrator. She can do this, but you don't need to do it in order to be supportive. Though overwhelmingly tempting this can be counter-productive, especially if she decides not to leave him at this time. Her feelings will be ambivalent and changeable. Condemn his behaviour, by all means, but be wary of condemning him until she is sure of her feelings and has safely separated.

What if I suspect abuse is happening?

What if you suspect domestic violence but are not sure? This calls for your best diplomatic and supportive skills. All the above advice applies in relation to listening and believing. Sometimes questions that are gentle and general are a good way to encourage someone to talk about this most painful situation. This could include:

'How are things between you and Xxxxx?'

'Are you worried about the children?'

'What do the arguments look like?'

'How are you coping?'

Take any fears very seriously because victims are usually the best assessors of their own safety. They will have a very detailed and nuanced understanding about his behaviour and when it is likely to escalate. They are the experts on his triggers, his manipulations, his mindset and his capacity for violence.

Extra risk factors

Some behavioural and situational factors are known to indicate extra risk.[2] They are:

- Past use of weapons in any domestic violence assault
- Current access to weapons
- Threats to kill the victim, family members or pets
- Threats or attempts by the perpetrator to commit suicide
- Stalking of the victim
- Sexual assault
- Drug and/or alcohol abuse
- Jealous and controlling behaviour
- Recent escalation of violence or threats
- The victim being pregnant

If the victim reports any of these or any other factor that she believes is a sign of danger, ask her what you can do to help. Support her in whatever steps she wants to take.

Try, above all, to leave her in charge. There is a saying to keep in mind that I call The Social Worker's Motto: People will insist on living their own lives, even when you know you'd do a much better job.

Supporting people who live with violence requires patience and care, often for a long time. Suspend your judgement, but not your concern for their welfare. She deserves safety, respect and support.

CHAPTER TEN
POSSIBILITIES FOR CHANGE

Can I get him to stop?

The short answer to this is, 'No, of course not.' Let us look again at what we know:

- If he is psychotic, he needs a medical assessment and treatment, and/or containment.
- It is most unlikely he is psychotic.
- If he is not, then he is choosing to behave like this. He wants to control or punish you and he doesn't care if that means hurting you or your children.
- You are not responsible for the violence, and no matter what you do he is likely to continue to be violent or controlling.
- You have probably already tried everything you can think of.

Of course, there are complexities. Like all behaviour, abusive behaviour is a continuum, from milder controlling behaviour to murderous intimate terrorism.

In my experience, men who abuse their partners never change if you ask them nicely. They do not change if you change, nor do they change if you plead, beg, argue your case for change or get their friends or big brothers to speak to them.

They change when they are made to (usually legally) or when they decide they want to. Some men move from partner to partner, ruining the happiness of a series of partners. They change partners, but not their behaviour.

If you are partnering with someone who disparages and vilifies his or her former partner, remember that you could be next.

Which men are unlikely to change?

- Men who do not believe they are to blame, and tell both their partner and themselves that it is her fault, or at least someone else is the cause.

- Men who are not motivated to change by negative consequences, like being charged with assault or being subject to a protective order.

- Men who say they can only change if their partner changes, too.

- Men who say they cannot change without you helping them. Often, this is a way to get you to stay in the relationship.

- Men who keep coming up with excuses about why they cannot seek help: they are too busy at work; too depressed; too damaged by their parents or they don't have enough money for therapy. If work is more important than your safety, or even the relationship, forget it. If they are depressed or 'damaged' then that is more of a reason to seek help. If cost is a problem, they should look for a low-fee government funded service.

- Men who insist that you trust them to change or forgive their past behaviour, or keep noticing every indicator of improvement. I have spoken to men who are indignant that their partner does not believe they are now safe to be with, even though they have treated her shockingly in the recent past.

- Men who want a guarantee you will stay with them, or return to them, if they seek help. In fact, if they are making any demands, they are unlikely to change.

- Men who point out previous abusive behaviour they are not doing any more. This is sometimes a threat that if you abandon him, he can always get nasty again. Think about it — if he is saying this, he is definitely nasty still.

- Men who expect sex as a right, available just because they want it.

- Men who are still frightening, threatening or intimidating you, even though they say they are changing.
- Men who are manipulative, and if you have left them keep manipulating the system to make your life difficult.

Which men are more likely to change?

Some men do change. Some are acting in ways they have learned, and they can and do learn to be non-abusive. Someone is moving towards being non-abusive when he can:

- Admit honestly how much he has hurt you and demonstrate an understanding of how much you and the children have suffered. When he can acknowledge the betrayal of trust, love and safety this represents and does not minimise or excuse his actions.
- Genuinely apologise, which in most cultures means making eye contact with those he has harmed, saying 'I am sorry' and pledging a commitment not to repeat his violence.
- Show empathy for you and for others.
- Admit and act to remedy mistakes in other areas of his life.
- Actively offer to make some restitution, such as the man who took an extra evening shift to pay for his former wife's counselling sessions.
- Show respect, both to you and to women in general. You might find he can listen to an alternative opinion you have that he does not agree with, without anger or interruption.
- Treat you as an independent equal. He no longer questions your movements or your decisions.
- Respect your wishes about sex, whatever they are, provided yours are respectful also. It is not disrespectful to say 'No' to sex.
- Take a more equal part in household and parenting responsibilities.

- Be aware of, and change, his bad habits such as eye-rolling, interrupting, checking up on you or being domineering in any way.

It is easy to become hopeful when change is what you want to see. A promise is not change, attendance at counselling or a group session is not change. Not all men who attend programs will change, in fact the research suggests fewer than half will.

If you cannot see change, it is not happening.

A life saver for men

In researching this book, I renewed my acquaintance with the Spousal Rate Of Killing statistics, an American set of data about intimate partner homicide. For many decades the United States had the dubious distinction of having a much higher rate of women killing their partners than other countries.

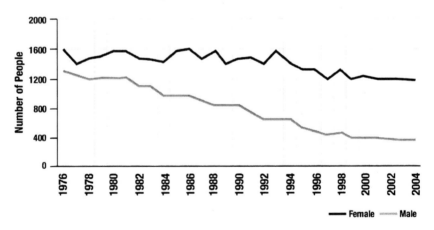

Intimate Partner Homicides by Gender
USA Crime Data 1976-2004

Table: USA male and female victims on intimate homicide, 1976-2005.[1]

Two researchers, Margo Wilson and Martin Daly, have studied this phenomenon. They found that over the 30 years since the advent of women's shelters in the 1970s something very interesting happened to the homicide statistics.

Between 1976 and 2005, the number of women killed by their male partners decreased by about 25 per cent, but the number of men killed by women dropped by 75 per cent.

This has saved the lives of nearly one thousand men every year. The main purpose of such shelters was to save women's lives, and it is hoped they have. An unexpected result is that they have been saving the lives of more men than women.

Why is this so? Martin and Daly[2] suggest that men and women kill their partners for different reasons. Men are more likely to kill their partners when they leave or soon after. Women more often kill their partner to stop the abuse. If they have an alternative, safe way to escape abuse they will take that option.

CHAPTER ELEVEN

GETTING OUT SAFELY

How do I know when I should get out? This is a very personal decision to make and only you can make it. You are the best judge of when you are safest to leave. You can get help and support in making this decision by talking to counsellors who understand intimate partner violence.

This will help you listen to your own wisdom about your safety, even though you may come to some painful realisations. These might include that he is not likely to change or that you may face many difficulties if you decide to leave the relationship, including increased abuse from your partner and discovering that the support you need is not always available in the community. These are some questions frequently asked by women wrestling with this decision.

When should I call the police?

Right across Australia there are now laws that mean police should protect victims of intimate partner violence. There are a number of things they should do.

- Police should respond promptly. This happens best when you call 000, so this is the number to call if you are concerned about your immediate safety or the safety of someone else. Calling the local police station or your local family violence service will not get the police to your door more quickly than if you call 000.

- Police can give you advice at a police station if you want to report an incident that has happened or a threat or other concern. Once there, you can ask to speak to a specially-trained family violence officer, if you wish.

- Call 000 if you are worried about the immediate physical safety of yourself, a family member, a neighbour or a stranger. This is much better than trying to intervene yourself.

What will the police do?

- Police are required to investigate reports and find out if a criminal offence, such as an assault, has been committed.
- Police will talk to all parties in a dispute. If they are called to an incident where there is a couple, they should speak to each person separately and out of earshot of the other.
- If police believe that a protective order should be taken out to help protect someone, they can do this. Read more about protective orders on page 103.
- Police can support people through the court process and can arrange an interpreter for court or to enable someone to make a statement. People involved in court matters will need to make a statement.
- In some areas police can now take video evidence at the scene, which can be used in court.
- Police complete a risk assessment process and will refer victims and perpetrators to services for support and help. This includes specialist domestic violence services, child protection services, men's behaviour change groups and counselling services.
- Police can help victims gather and download evidence, such as threatening phone calls or text messages.

Police take an oath that means that if they believe a crime has been committed they need to act. This means that once you ask police for help, they will decide to take action as they see fit.

In recent decades police view intimate partner violence more often as a crime, not just a private matter and this is a very good thing. Although the police response has improved in many areas and ways, there are still times when women wish they had not raised the alarm because they do not feel supported by police. There are still infrequent occasions when police do not or cannot attend, and there are still some police who do not really understand the issues. This is especially distressing as it can often increase the danger to the victim.

Even when police commence well, sometimes investigations or court-related support is not followed up, or not done in a timely manner.

A recent case in the media demonstrated this when a woman who was to give evidence against her violent former partner was arrested and detained for days after she failed to appear in court because she was unaware the court date had been set.

Prosecutors then opposed bail, arguing she may not attend court if she was released.[1]

How can I get out?

Leaving a relationship where you are being treated badly is rarely simple and it can be very dangerous. Many women are unaware that there are services to help someone who is living with an abusive partner. There is a 24-hour national hotline called 1800 Respect (1800 737 732) that covers the whole of Australia and can direct you to local services.

There are also some excellent smartphone apps. Check out the resources section at the back of this book.

Of course, there is never enough funding for these services and even the national hotline estimated that they had 18,000 unanswered calls to their service in 2014.[2]

Keep persevering, or call your local community health service or police station and ask for the number of the closest domestic violence support service.

Be aware that even men who have not used physical violence before can become dangerous when they think, or find out, that you are planning to leave.

It is much better to make a planned exit with the best information and support you can find than an emergency exit in a crisis.

In other words, if you can, it is better to plan your path to safety and think through what you need to do to make this happen. Family violence specialists call this safety planning.

Safety plans

If you are thinking of leaving a relationship where you are unsafe, put as much in place as you can to help your escape.

- Go and speak to a domestic violence worker, or call a hotline. A face-to-face meeting is better and you can hear about different services and decide which ones you will need. You might need help with housing or information about social security benefits.

- There are special payments and support for people escaping violence.

- Get legal advice and get it early. I know many women who believed their partners when they were told complete lies about their legal rights. For example, you might be told that the house is not in your name, so 'you will not get a thing'. Or that you will never get custody of your children because you are not working, or you have had depression. While these threats should be nonsense (legally), court outcomes can never be assumed. Until all courts have a consistently better record of ensuring the safety of victims and until the judicial system does a better job of holding perpetrators to account, there will be some unjust and dangerous outcomes. A local community legal service can assist you with information and usually a free session to help you understand what you need to know. There are often conflict of interest issues in family matters. If your partner has sought legal aid or sought help from a lawyer you already know then you usually cannot get help from the same legal centre or lawyer. If you have a family lawyer, only see them if you absolutely trust their discretion and integrity. If they play golf with your partner, forget it and get some independent advice.

- In other words, make sure your lawyer is impartial and informed about domestic violence.

- Check out your house and have an emergency exit plan. Make note of whether some places are safer than others and where there are phones, exits and weapons. Walk through your emergency exit plan. One woman told me how she left her front security door unlocked so she could run out the door and drive off if she was being attacked. The first time she tried this, she ran out and then realised her car keys were on a hook in the kitchen. You may need to have a special place for your phone and a second car key. I have heard more than one young woman say that she knows when an assault is imminent because her partner takes her phone.

- Have your own bank account. If you do not have one, you will need a birth certificate or passport and other documents to establish your ID. Try to get some money together in case you need it.

- Pack a bag of things you need every day and hide it. I have had clients keep such a bag with a friend or relative they trust, or in a hiding spot such as under the house. One woman told me she had sprayed a garbage bag heavily inside and out with insecticide to keep out the spiders and put her escape bag into this. She added grimly, 'I used most of the can. If he doesn't kill me, the Mortein might.'

- If you have friends or family you can really trust, you might want to pre-organise a signal or code word that lets them know you need help. Perhaps you could 'prank call' them, or have a special phrase you will need if you want them to come or call the police. One has to admire the woman who kept her friend's number saved as 'veterinarian' and arranged to message her when she needed police, using the word 'rabies'. This woman's partner was eventually charged with her attempted murder when he tried to strangle her; she regained consciousness on the kitchen floor after he thought she was dead.

- Create a list of important phone numbers from police to grandma, your lawyer, doctor, child's school and any of your support services. Keep this list safe and if you can, leave a copy with a trusted friend.

- Collect important documents or make copies. A sample list would include:
  » Birth certificate
  » Passport
  » Banking information, account numbers and passwords
  » Tax returns
  » School reports

- » Qualifications
- » Car registration certificate
- » Information for government agencies, such as Centrelink
- » Medical information, including Medicare
- » Insurance paperwork
- » Mortgage paperwork
- » Jewellery that means a lot to you
- » Photos and mementos that mean a lot to you
- » Things your children need, such as immunisation records
- » Prescriptions
- Take your computer, if you have one and you can. Change your passwords often. Be computer savvy. These days, many women are stalked after they leave, and this is usually through their phone settings or the GPS in their car. Read about cyber safety before you leave or get some advice from one of the services funded to help you with tech safety.[3]
- Think through what you need for your children and what they might need to do in an emergency, if they are old enough.
- Keep a journal while you are planning to leave and after you have left, until you are completely safe.
- This is not a journal about your feelings, just keep a record of incidents as soon as possible after they occur such as threats, assaults or what a lawyer or police member promises to do. This can be very useful in keeping track of what is happening and can be used as evidence in court, if necessary. You will always know when child contact was cancelled, how many phone calls you got 'that night:' whether your partner saw the children on his birthday or what happened before or after an incident; these are the sorts of details that are often disputed.

If possible, it is good to link in with a case worker in a community agency or domestic violence service when planning to exit a relationship with someone who uses violence.

A case worker will have no trouble understanding your experiences, having heard many similar accounts, and can help you both navigate the system and advocate for you within it (police/courts/housing services) if the system seems to be letting you down.

Protective orders

In different parts of the country, protective orders may be called Intervention Orders, an Apprehended Domestic Violence Order or an Order of Protection.

The purpose of such an order is to set in place conditions that a person must not breach, for the safety of the protected person. It is a civil order made by the court to protect a family member from another person. Police can apply for such an order to protect someone, or people can apply themselves. The proportion of such orders taken out by police varies from state to state. In Victoria, where police can apply for an order — even if the victim does not wish them to — about 70 per cent are taken out by police.

These civil orders send a message to the person who has used violence that the matter is being taken seriously, and when police take out such an order it is a positive symbol of the community's censure of the violence. It is often easier for a person when police apply for an order because there is less onerous paperwork and they cannot be blamed by the perpetrator for taking them to court.

A protective order restricts someone from certain offensive types of behaviour. The magistrate can add conditions that are seen to be necessary. These might include:

- Not being within a certain distance from the victim
- Staying away from particular locations, such as a workplace
- Not contacting the victim
- Not damaging property
- Not instructing anyone else to commit any stalking, harassing or violent behaviour against the victim
- Staying in the same house, but not being allowed to harass or harm the victim

It is important to remember to add the names of any dependent children to the order who also need protection from violence. This rarely happens by default, even if the perpetrator has harmed them directly in the past. If you are staying at a new and secret location, this information should not be stated on the application forms or the orders issued at court. It is also important to check the spelling of everyone's names on the order before leaving court after the hearing, so as to prevent perpetrators from claiming that the order does not relate to you or to them.

A protective order is not a criminal matter, it is a civil matter. This means that the respondent (the person whose behaviour is limited by the order) is not being charged with anything and will not have a criminal record.

A criminal record can affect a person's ability to work in certain professions, or travel internationally, but this is not the case with protective orders. In most Australian states a protective order cancels a person's firearms licence and police can remove any guns registered to their name.

A protective order works in cases where the respondent does not want to have a criminal record, which might eventuate if the order is breached. However, if the respondent does not care about the consequences then a protective order can be worthless. Anyone who has a protective order put in place still needs to be very vigilant about their safety.

If your Order of Protection is breached you should immediately report this to the police and keep any evidence you have, such as text messages or emails.

There are some good websites that can help you understand protective orders and breaches, including legal aid and community legal websites. The 1800 Respect website has links to information about these orders in every Australian state. For more information, see the Resources section for the 1800respect website.

Family mediation and dispute resolution

In Australia, it is mandatory for most couples applying to the Family Court of Australia to have a certificate from a family relationship or legal aid centre to confirm that they have attended mediation.

The aim is to try to settle issues before starting legal action. Where there has been domestic violence or a partner will not attend mediation, a mediator can issue a certificate indicating this so that the remaining partner can apply to court to settle the issues. Mediation is not intended to be counselling for couples or to try to repair the relationship.

Attending mediation does not mean you have to attend on the same day as your partner, and you can also talk to the centre about being in separate rooms if you do attend on the same day, which is called 'shuttle mediation'.

You can refuse mediation if you are too afraid of your partner to attend at all, but it is best to talk to a mediator first, on your own, if this is the case.

Some perpetrators use mediation to try to pressure victims to renew the relationship or to threaten them in relation to child contact, and mediators need to be aware of such tactics.

Some perpetrators may deliberately draw out the process by cancelling appointments or demand frequent breaks or extended time with the mediator.

It is important to speak to a legal advisor to prepare for mediation, and if necessary a domestic violence support service.

Criminal charges

There are significant differences between a civil protective order and a criminal charge.

A protective order is to restrict a person's behaviour. A criminal charge is to make a person accountable for breaking the law, and to punish him or her if they are found guilty. A protective order has conditions while a successfully prosecuted criminal charge results in a conviction.

The level of proof for a court to make a protective order is the balance of probability, whereas a criminal charge must be proved beyond reasonable doubt. Finally, while a victim can seek a protective order, it is almost always police who pursue criminal charges.

For many centuries domestic violence was not treated as a crime. In a sense, society is still catching up with changes to the law that have criminalised domestic violence in recent decades. For example, it was not until the 1980s that laws in Australia changed to allow for the fact that the crime of rape could occur within marriage.

Having charges laid does not always lead to a conviction, and victims are often disappointed with court outcomes.

The New South Wales Bureau of Crime Statistics and Research studied 20,000 cases of domestic violence related offences from 2008-2010.[4]

They found that the most common penalty for a domestic violence offence is a bond. An unsupervised bond is also the most common sentence for those convicted of stalking.

Most of the offenders who were not jailed received no supervision of their sentence and no requirement to attend men's behaviour change programs or counselling.

It is little wonder that the incidence of reoffending is so high. Survivors made some harrowing submissions to the Victorian Royal Commission into Family Violence. One woman catalogued some of the abuse she had suffered over years, including many physical and sexual assaults. Here is an excerpt from one brave survivor:

- 'Smashing my head against walls'
- 'Whilst going to the toilet he would push me off my seat'
- 'Pushing me over in the shower'
- 'Verbal threats and calling me names'
- 'Saying he would bury me in a hole and threatening to shoot me'

On one occasion this woman was most viciously assaulted over many hours. Her partner threatened to kill her and she believed she was going to die. She managed to call for help, and was taken to hospital. Her partner was arrested and charged with grievous bodily harm. In court, he received a 12-month suspended sentence.[5]

There are many instances that parallel this, as well as those where men have killed their partners and been found guilty of manslaughter, not murder. I have supported women in court where their partners have been found guilty of, or pleaded guilty to, serious assaults and walked out with a bond or a fine.

If the law is going to treat domestic violence as any other crime that should include treating the place where an assault takes place as a crime scene and being conscientious about collecting and storing evidence.

It means that courts will look at the history of the offender before sentencing and give a meaningful sentence.

It means recognising that past behaviour is an indicator of future behaviour and that a sentence needs to send the clear message that violence is not excusable.

In the Family Court reports of intimate partner violence, even when evidence is clear, are not always dealt with as if they are crimes.

CHAPTER TWELVE

THE FAMILY COURT

The Family Court is the area of the community's response to intimate partner violence that is most fraught with heartache and controversy. Family violence is the 'bread and butter' of Family Court business. A very high proportion of cases heard in the Family Court involve allegations of abuse or violence.[1]

The Family Court's core business

Family law is intended to prioritise the best interests of children when their parents separate and to resolve property disputes.

In relation to children, the two primary criteria are that children should have a meaningful relationship with both their parents and that children should be protected from harm and abuse. Unfortunately, these basic principles soon come into conflict when a child has a parent who uses violence, abuse or coercion to achieve their ends.

Reasonable, loving parents who put the needs of their children first do apply these principles. Many parents who separate sort out their parenting arrangements and finances themselves or with the help of a lawyer.

Unfortunately, there are also a lot of women leaving a relationship with someone who is coercive and controlling who are bullied into settling out of court.

Where there is a pattern of abuse, and especially where the perpetrator tries to use the legal system to continue to control and abuse his former partner, cases can drag on for years.

Few people realise that most of the cases (79 per cent) dealt with in the Family Court involve allegations of a history of abuse, usually of the mother or the children or both.[2]

This should lead to a development of considerable understanding about family violence within the court system, but in some cases it seems to have had the opposite effect.

Instead of realising that this is a huge problem which needs to be addressed, there have been responses that indicate that the prevalence of the issue is interpreted as meaning it cannot be happening, or if it is the court cannot prevent it.

Some victims are told by lawyers or the court that violence perpetrated against them is in the past or otherwise irrelevant to the perpetrator's capacity to parent.

An article in *The Monthly* by Jess Hill reported that Professor Patrick Parkinson, former chair of the Family Law Council, said he was worried about how often mothers were losing custody of their children after alleging or disclosing abuse.[3]

'Some lawyers now tell their clients, "If you make these allegations, you risk losing the care of your child", he said.

Allegations of abuse

In 2013, Justice David Collier commented that mothers were increasingly making up allegations of abuse of their children to stop fathers from seeing their children.[4]

In 2014, the Chief Justice of the Family Court, Diana Bryant, was quoted on ABC radio as saying that 'violent parents are often granted some level of access to children, subject to risk assessment'.

She said that when it comes to violence there's only so much the law can do.[5]

Fiona McCormack, head of Domestic Violence Victoria, responded to this comment: 'I think we need to be asking, and particularly child protection and the Family Law Court need to really be thinking much more about when parents who choose to use violence, at what point do they actually forfeit their rights to have access to their children?'[6]

It is a common experience that many women who leave a partner because of family violence, and report that violence to the court, face a difficult time.

Abuse often escalates following separation. The adversarial nature of the court processes make it much more suited to those who have well-developed tactics for asserting their power and control and have the resources to use such tactics.

It works against those who are emerging from a situation of fear and trauma where giving in to intimidation has been a matter of their, and their children's, survival. Study after study show that women and children escaping domestic violence receive less in property settlements[7] and little or no child support[8] and that child contact becomes an opportunity for perpetrators to continue harassment and abuse.[9]

Australian research by Elspeth McInnes in 2004 confirmed a phenomenon of which domestic violence workers and victims are well aware, that leaving a relationship with someone who is abusive often involves a rapid and deep slide into poverty.

Not only that, there is no such slide if you are a perpetrator. In fact, a perpetrator with the help of the court systems can often extract from the victim the little wealth they have.[10]

The conflict that is the hallmark of a relationship with an abuser can be replicated in a Family Court battle with the woman having to prove the abuse. Abuse, manipulation and intimidation can continue throughout the court process and beyond.

As one woman said, 'I now feel safe in my home, but I do not feel safe in the system.'

A hallmark of domestic violence is the harm caused to the mother-child (or parent-child) relationship. Perpetrators may create allies of the children to support their abuse.

A report produced by the Domestic Violence Resource Centre, Victoria, in 2009 (Bad Mothers and Invisible Fathers) looked at the parenting of fathers who had a history of perpetrating violence against their partners.

They found studies indicating that such men are more likely to use physical or harsh discipline, and to abuse their children in a number of ways.[11]

More is required for good parenting than merely an absence of violence. Mothers are often told by child protection workers to leave relationships with men who are violent, or their children may be placed in foster care. Shortly after she does so, the Family Court can require her to make an agreement for contact arrangements with the same man.

We know that few women have a documented history of their abuse, and most abuse is not reported. Protective orders are not regarded as proof of abuse having occurred.

Even if the evidence is accepted, it is not always recognised that this indicates a risk of future abuse or a lack of capacity to provide adequate care for the children.

Some decisions indicate that the court is under the false belief that a man who has consistently harmed or terrorised his partner can readily be expected to be a loving and positive parent.

This can lead to huge problems. Mothers who are reporting concerns about the sexual abuse of their children often request that the children not spend time unsupervised with the perpetrator. If that is their father, the mother can be seen as not facilitating a relationship between the child and their father. Leading psychologists and psychiatrists sometimes recommend that the children in such circumstances be removed from their mother's care and only allowed minimal contact with her, and placed fulltime with the father.

You might think these cases would be followed up to make sure the children are safe. But this does not happen. The case is over and the court and the professionals involved hope they got it right.

In June, 2015, the ABC show *Background Briefing* covered this issue.[12] It made for disturbing listening. One woman who was interviewed said that despite disclosing that her father was sexually abusing her, she was ordered to have weekend contact with him where the abuse continued unabated. This arrangement had been recommended by a Family Court Assessment report.

Assessments for court

Assessing people for court is a demanding area of work and requires experience, knowledge and sensitivity. Among the pitfalls in conducting respectful assessments are the biases of the assessor, which can easily influence the recommendations made.

An example from my own practice concerns the gender-stereotyped attitude that sees women as the necessary nurturers with primary responsibility for the welfare of children and the success of relationships.

A case of gender bias:

Whose job is it to guarantee a child's safety?

Dr P, a male psychiatrist was doing an assessment for court of the D Family, Penny (mum), Anthony (dad) and the two children, Tyla and Davo. The mother, Penny D, had been referred to counselling by a women's refuge. Dr P rang me because I was Penny's counsellor. He said he felt that Penny's mental health was fragile, and he would therefore recommend that the children be placed with Anthony.

I asked Dr P if he was concerned about the long and established history of violence perpetrated by Anthony, including chasing the children around the house with a machete.

He replied that he had interviewed Anthony's new partner Donna, and thought she was 'pretty much together'.

This was unfair to both Penny, whose fragile mental health was likely to improve now that she was no longer being routinely assaulted, and to Donna who was clearly now expected to be the main protector of this man's children.

Tyla and Davo eventually endured a traumatic removal by police due to their father's continued violence.

When interviewing parents I always ask about details of the child's daily life, such as the name of their favourite teacher, who are their best friends and to describe their last play date. Parents who really know and talk to their children can readily answer such questions.

Another example of personal gender bias would be when a man is seen as more believable and logical, valuing the supremacy of presenting as rational and unemotional, and the woman seen as too emotional or 'flaky'.

In such a case conditions may be set by the court that reflect that the woman not the man needs help, or disregard the fact that the man uses violence.

Consider this real example:

Who needs to do the work: When there is violence who needs to address their issues?

Luke had a long history post-separation of harassing and threatening his ex-wife, Elizabeth, by refusing to pay child support and often not returning the children after access. Intervention orders against him were in place.

The Family Court ordered a psychiatric assessment of the family. Dr B, who had provided many reports to court, did this assessment.

Dr B's report noted that neither parent met the DSM-V13 criteria for any disorder, but he said that the assessment had raised concerns about Elizabeth being anxious and depressed to some degree. This was no surprise to me, given what she had survived. Dr B did note that Elizabeth had reported that Luke frequently lost his temper with the children, and had once ripped off kitchen cupboard doors in a rage. He concluded that Luke 'may have difficulty managing his frustration and anger when upset by the behaviour of others'.

Recommendations from that report were eventually incorporated into the Parenting Orders, and they required that Elizabeth undergo another psychiatric assessment and seek medical and psychological support for her anxiety and depression.

No recommendations were made in relation to Luke's mental health or problems with anger.

Family Court Assessments

In the 2014 Victorian Community attitudes survey, 48 per cent of people believed that women make up or exaggerate claims of domestic violence to gain increased custody or contact with their children.[14]

This is another example of an incorrect and dangerous community attitude. A 2003 Family Court Review found that while mothers were twice as likely as fathers to notify family courts of child abuse concerns, mothers' concerns were four times as likely to be substantiated by the court compared to a father's allegations.

So, what does it matter if the public have the wrong idea? It matters because lawyers, Family Court Assessment writers and the judiciary, can hold these attitudes.

As a psychologist, I am interested in assessments and have thought about what needs to be considered when doing such assessments. I certainly see the past abuse of a partner as a risk factor to consider when making a recommendation about child contact.

It is vital that assessors explore a perpetrator's capacity to admit and acknowledge abuse that has occurred, and that it was a choice, their choice. It is important that people who have used violence demonstrate a capacity to accept responsibility and to understand that their partners and children have been affected, and also that it may take a long time to recover a sense of trust and safety with them.

Anyone doing such an assessment should be looking to discover whether perpetrators can understand and relinquish their destructive sense of entitlement, and how they can reassure the community that their children will be safe in their care.

If an abusive parent minimises their violence or an assessor disregards reports of violence from women and children, this is a sign that they have a poor understanding of violent behaviour and the dynamics of intimate partner abuse.

Parental alienation

Some women have had truly awful experiences when they report the sexual abuse of their children. They have ended up losing the care of their children to the person the child says is sexually abusing them.

It is very difficult to establish that you are acting protectively in not wanting your child to have contact with an ex-partner.

Some assessment report writers are convinced that there are cases where the child may only seem to be afraid of a parent about whom they have disclosed abuse. They recommend that the child be placed full-time with that parent, so that the child will come to learn they are safe. The recommendation means that child is removed from the parent who is their primary carer, even though no concerns are raised about that parent except that they are reporting sexual abuse.

The biggest problem with such cases is that if abuse is occurring, it will continue without any protection for the child. Compounding this, once such a Parenting Order is made, there is usually no follow-up required to see how these children are going and whether they are, in fact, safe.

The thinking behind these decisions is based on the concept of 'parental alienation syndrome', a controversial concept suggested by an American psychiatrist in the 1980s. Neither the American Psychiatric Association nor the American Medical Association have recognised it as a syndrome. It has been criticised as having no scientific basis.[15]

This concept describes a situation where a child denigrates a parent without justification because it is claimed the child has been indoctrinated, or that one parent (usually the mother) has deliberately influenced the child against the other parent as part of a custody dispute. This is not recognised as a legitimate disorder or as a concept with any empirical basis in courts in Australia, or elsewhere.

Sometimes the term 'parental alienation' is still used to indicate that a child denigrates one parent because they have been coached or persuaded to do so by the other. Unfortunately, this can lead to children's reports of abuse or evident distress in the company of a parent to be discounted. This is because 'parental alienation' often relies on the claim that it can be caused by a parent's subconscious or unconscious desires.

This is a tangled web for Family Court report writers, as well as for judges and magistrates. The follow-up of children placed with parents who have been accused of violence against them would be an excellent starting point for research into the outcomes of these children. This follow-up would need to continue into adult life, at least until the age of 25, when the person feels able to freely speak about their experience of the court decisions made in their name.

Independent children's lawyers

In the Family Court, children are represented by an Independent Children's Lawyer (ICL) who is charged with the task of representing the children's interests in court. Sadly, most children have never met or even spoken to their lawyer.

A study by the Australian Institute of Family Studies painted a very poor picture of the ICL process and concluded that the ICLs provided a 'poor representation of children's best interests'.[16]

They found that only 12 per cent of ICLs had interviewed the child separately from their parents, and that 38 per cent of ICLs had not interviewed any of the parties at all!

It is hard to understand how they can be regarded as representing these children.

I have been told by more than one ICL that they rely heavily on the Family Court Assessment Report, as does the judge or magistrate.

Do Family Court decisions protect children?

There is no doubt that sometimes the Family Court does protect children from an abusive parent, but there is plenty of evidence emerging that this is not always the case.

I have spoken to women who have been told by lawyers, family report writers and by magistrates that the violence done to them is 'in the past'. They are told, it is 'not related to his contact with the children'. They are even told, 'If you keep bringing this up, it won't help you in court.'

There is more research overseas about outcomes for children when the Family Court fails to believe mothers about the danger to themselves and their children.

Joan Meier is the director of the Domestic Violence Legal Empowerment and Appeals Project in the USA. In an article in the *Journal of Child Custody* in 2009, she found that when she searched 'all electronically available opinions regarding custody and claims of parental alienation during a 10-year period, she found that fathers brought 82 per cent of alienation claims which they won nearly 70 per cent of the time, meaning that in those cases, mothers lost primary custody'.[17]

An article in the *Boston Globe* in January, 2016, discussed cases where children have been exposed to serious and repeated harm when the court does not believe reports of violence.[18]

They report that court decisions can be fatal. The article referred to a US 2013 study that 'found 175 documented cases during a two-year period where children were killed by their fathers after courts refused the mother's requests to ensure that paternal visitation was supervised or eliminated'.

The *Background Briefing* episode referred to earlier gives us no reason to think that the situation is very different in Australia.

In 2009, an article in *The Australian* reported that Judge Paul Cronin had criticised a mother for not ensuring her children had contact visits with their father even if the children refused to go.

'While parents don't have to "physically drag" the children to the other parent, they do have to "positively encourage" them to go, and punish those who refuse,' the judge said.[19]

In December, 2015, *The Australian* reported on another judge's decision: 'A seven-year-old girl has been allowed to live with her father despite making "multiple disclosures" of sexual abuse by him, including that he hurt her by touching her "in the wrong places".'[20]

Most of us are familiar with cases of children who have been killed by their fathers on access visits, in spite of reports of the father being dangerous.[21]

These children include Darcy Freeman, Luke Batty and Asia, Jarius and Grace Osborne.

As a child psychologist who sees children who are fearful of a parent, the outcomes can be extraordinarily heart-breaking. Children talk about wondering where they can hide to avoid access visits; how to be brave when they are so afraid, or ask why they and their protective parent cannot just 'run away'.

The current situation is this:

- The Family Court does not have the resources to investigate allegations of abuse.
- The children involved are barely consulted by the Family Court.
- Some people with influential positions in the Family Court may have beliefs about allegations and abuse that are incorrect and could put a child in danger.
- This leaves children who are victims of abuse in a position where a group of powerful professionals in the Family Court are making life-changing decisions about them, yet there is little consultation with them.

- The Family Court system not only risks disadvantaging victims, it has no mechanism to follow up its decisions and learn from them.

We have learned so much about the damage that is caused when victims are not believed.

The Royal Commission into Institutional Responses to Child Sexual Abuse has shown this starkly. The public are shocked not just by the nature of these children's experiences, but also by the fact that if they did speak up, they were invariably not believed. There are many victims who feel this way about the Family Court, and have done so for decades. It is vital that women involved with the Family Court have access to good legal advice and a lawyer they can trust who understands intimate partner violence.

Where does a broke and broken woman get adequate legal advice? This has always been difficult and with cutbacks to legal aid over the last few years, it is often impossible.

It is so important that perpetrators are held accountable by all the community, and especially by the courts.

When courts fail to see a pattern in the behaviour of the perpetrator, minimise individual incidents or see individual incidents in isolation rather than as part of a pattern, then child and adult victims will continue to be harmed. When the abuse of one parent by the other is discounted, children will remain at risk in their care.

A judge's sobering moment

In 2014, I attended a family violence forum and heard a woman tell a harrowing but familiar tale about her struggle to get justice in the Family Court, including her ex-partner hiding assets, refusing to pay child support, and denying a history of violence in spite of a number of police callouts to their home.

She spoke about feeling unsupported by the system and being terrified in the Family Court just to be in a corridor with her ex-partner. Afterwards, I spoke to a family court judge who also attended. The judge commented that they would like to be able to speak to that woman and let her know that she should not have had such a struggle, and that the system had clearly let her down. The judge seemed taken aback when I said that this woman was not an isolated case, that there were literally thousands of women with similar stories.

There are good judges and magistrates doing their best.
They need to track and listen to the survivors of the system.

Why courts need angels

One of the programs I started is a mentoring program that trains volunteers and matches them with domestic violence survivors for a year, to share the journey of recovery.[22] This program has been highly successful in terms of the mental health and safety outcomes for women in the program. The mentor 'angel' can stop in regularly for a chat, and can attend appointments or court with the woman.

When evaluating this program, I asked one survivor what difference it had made to her having a mentor. She told me the story of being on her own one day at the Family Court, shuffling between meetings with lawyers while trying to reach an agreement about child contact. During the lunch break, she was sitting in a waiting area when her ex-husband came past, looking like a smartly dressed businessman. She shrank back, but he leaned over and whispered in her ear what she called a 'disgusting threat'. He walked on and she sat there shaking and tearful.

She told her lawyer about the incident and he brought it up when the legal round of mediation started again. The ex-husband denied it vehemently, and said that his ex-wife 'makes up stuff like this all the time'.

The woman told me: 'If I had an angel with me, that would never have happened.'

This story says so much about how the system fails victims, disbelieving them, exposing them to further abuse and then being unable to recognise it.

CHAPTER THIRTEEN
WHAT HELPS RECOVERY?

Practical support

There are specialist services that can assist women living with violence, but they differ in what they can offer. This is due to the history of the various services and to the funding they receive. Some help with housing, some specialise in women's refuges and emergency housing, and some with case management — they link you to the services you need. Unfortunately, there are a number of services but not an integrated service system, so finding what you need can be extremely stressful.

To discover what services are near you, go to the 1800 RESPECT website and look for services in your state. Navigating the system to find the best services for your situation can be tricky, but it is well worth it.

The availability of practical support varies enormously between and within states, so look for a service with experience in family violence that can help you find out what is available. Many survivors seek help from counsellors or support groups. These options can be very helpful.

Individual counselling

Individual counselling can help sort out your next steps and allows you to talk about and reflect on your personal experiences. It can give you the space to plan, and to build up your confidence and courage.

In my experience, if women are supported respectfully by someone who understands their experience they will make good decisions for themselves and their children.

Find a counsellor with a good understanding of the dynamics of family violence and a belief in your personal autonomy. Do not settle for anyone who tells you what to do — you've had more than enough of that! Especially steer clear of a counsellor who in any way excuses or explains the abuse or judges your responses negatively.

If you are unhappy with your counsellor and do not feel supported, remember that it is a service and you are the customer. Find another counsellor. Your safety and recovery are too important to be compromised.

Support groups

Domestic violence support groups provide education about domestic violence to women survivors in a group setting and women can support each other through sharing experiences of recovery. Group support provides the added advantage of getting support from other women who understand at least some of what you have been through and how you feel. The women attending these groups may have had similar experiences which can be very helpful in understanding that you were not the problem, and they will also share information about what has helped them survive and thrive.

Facilitators of these groups often have long experience in supporting women to support each other, and these groups also involve information about how to help you and your children recover.

Why couple counselling cannot help

Couple counselling can help with issues such as parenting, communication, differing family expectations, grief, problems with in-laws or major life decisions and transitions.

As a therapist, I have found it is a beautiful privilege to help a couple rediscover the love they once had, and find ways to make their home and family life more joyful. Couples who have had troubling experiences can support each other in moving and humbling ways.

Seeing a couple therapist can help when couples have an equal relationship but it cannot help where there is domestic violence. For counselling to be useful, everyone needs to feel safe enough to say whatever they need to say, without fear or favour. If you can't do that counselling is pointless and it is a ripe ground for manipulation, coercion, intimidation and attempts to find fault in the victim.

If the dynamic in the couple relationship is such that one person is dominating, coercing, intimidating or hurting the other, the victim will not be safe to say what she needs. In such a relationship, couple therapy can be dangerous.

Therapists do not always understand this and hope they can help pour oil on troubled waters. They might ask both partners to change. This is just what the abusive partner wants; he believes she is partly or wholly to blame all along. The therapist might foster sympathy for the abusive partner because of his depression, his childhood or some such factor. None of this will help the non-abusive partner, but it could make it worse for her.

The therapist might collude with the abusive partner and make it all about the woman's depression or parenting style. Reputable couple counsellors assess for domestic violence and usually have a session with each partner individually as part of the assessment at the beginning of the process. If there is abuse, couple counselling is not the place to deal with it. The partners should be referred to suitable individual alternatives.

The victim may benefit from individual counselling or a support group. The abusive partner should make their way to a reputable, long-term men's behaviour change program.

CHAPTER FOURTEEN
WHAT'S GENDER GOT TO DO WITH IT?

Minding our language

My long exposure to domestic violence has taught me the important relationship between language and attitude.

Community attitudes about a topic are reflected in the language used, and sometimes words that seem innocuous become associated with positive or negative judgements about what they describe.

One example of the association between language and attitudes to men and women is the words used for unmarried men and women. The word 'bachelor' signifies a man who does not identify as having an exclusive sexual partner, a single man. What adjectives come to your mind when you think of a bachelor? Perhaps single, young, eligible, independent or even dashing or handsome?

The equivalent word for an unmarried woman is 'spinster'. What adjectives come to mind when you hear that word? Perhaps an older woman comes to mind, someone frustrated or an 'old maid'? The *Oxford American English Dictionary* states: 'In modern everyday English spinster … is a derogatory term alluding to the stereotype of an older woman who is unmarried, childless, prissy and repressed.'

'Well, thanks very much,' I can hear some of my friends saying. Now, for another example, think of a four-letter word starting with 's' for someone who enjoys lots of casual sex. Were you thinking of a 'stud' or a 'slut'? Decide whether you think each of these is a positive or negative term. Why is it that men are invariably the studs and women are usually the sluts, when talking about similar sexual behaviour?

There are many other examples of ways in which language reflects different standards for, or treatment of, men and women — thereby revealing how society treats men and women differently. I recall the introduction of the word 'Ms' as an alternative to 'Miss' or 'Mrs', to combat the practice of a person's marital status being defined in their title. I remember being called a 'career girl' but never heard of anyone being called a 'career boy'.

I have often been asked how I manage to juggle the demands of practising a profession with raising my children. My husband has never once been asked that question. All these examples reflect the standards and expectations society places on men and women.

Let's look at the language people use when talking about relationships where there is domestic violence. It is very common to hear of a couple having an 'abusive relationship'.

I never use that term. A relationship is something mutual, it requires some level of agreement and reciprocity. When one person hurts or dominates another, especially when they relate to them in a pattern of hurt or domination, then that is not a mutual relationship. The real problem I have with the term 'abusive relationship' is that it sounds as if both parties contribute to the abuse, and that lets the person who is using violence off the hook.

Violence is a choice; it is a unilateral, not a mutual, action. In fact, if we do not believe violence is a choice, how are we going to change those terrible statistics?

Once a relationship is categorised as abusive, the abuse seems all too inevitable. It also implies that victims of violence could be doing something to stop the violence occurring if they wanted to, once again diluting the responsibility of the perpetrator. So, let's talk about a relationship where someone is using violence or abuse and name it for what it is, which is intimate partner violence. Let's not call it an abusive relationship.

Language and crime

For many decades, a major concern of those campaigning to reduce family violence has been society's failure to treat intimate partner crimes in the same way as other crimes.

In intimate partner assaults the victim may be urged to return to the person who has just assaulted them, or made to negotiate or mediate with someone who has raped or tortured them. One way to appreciate this difference is to imagine what it would sound like to use the language common to domestic crimes in other crime situations.

Imagine the following scenarios:

Mr Busy reports that he has been robbed 19 times by his neighbour, George. Mr Busy says he has not always called the police because they seemed to be able to do little to help. The magistrate fined George $100 and put him on a good behaviour bond. He recommended that Mr Busy keep in touch with George because they have lots of mutual friends in the neighbourhood.

Or this:

Harry's behaviour seems to have improved since he has been attending a program called 'Making Change, Not Stealing It'.

He said he does not understand why he is still banned from going to his local liquor store where he threatened the manager with a knife last Christmas, before breaking a bottle of beer over his head and robbing him.

He wants the manager to attend a Trust and Reconciliation Program with him as he feels it will help them both get closure about the incident and renew their relationship.

Gender and equality

There is a growing debate about the relevance of gender equality, or gender equity, to a discussion about domestic violence. What is meant by gender equality, and what does it have to do with domestic violence? Is there a link between the oppression of women in a community and the prevalence of domestic violence in that community? Gender equality is about fairness, it is about a lack of any discrimination based on gender. It means that whether you are a woman or a man (or transgender) you have the same human rights, the same right to opportunities, education, political power and the right to make decisions about your own life.

Sadly, there are still children, women and men across the world who live as slaves, and this is a disgrace. There is still gross inequality in opportunity and education in some countries. There have been centuries of struggle for women to gain the most basic equal rights, such as equal pay for equal work, the right to vote or to attend university, or to become a doctor or a plumber.

Women can now own property, rather than be property. Unfortunately, complete gender equality has not yet been achieved in any nation, and existing inequalities are very persistent. We are trying to change a social order that has been unchanged for centuries, but which actively discriminates against women.

When more effort is put into treating women and men equally, rates of violence against women in that community are lower.[1]

World Health Organisation and the United Nations research has found that where gender inequalities are most evident, there are also the highest rates of violence against women.[2]

In my experience as a psychologist and domestic violence counsellor, I have found the incidence of intimate partner violence to be very gendered in its occurrence.

Unfortunately, most societies across the world are still organised in ways that privilege men. Men earn more income, own and inherit more property and have more freedom.

Women have been regarded as property for most of history, and only in the last few hundred years, in some countries, have they been able to inherit property in the same way men can. Most women can now vote (and wasn't that a momentous battle) and earn a living in the same way a man can. However, there is still a significant disparity between male and female wages: in Australia women earn an average wage that is 17.9 per cent lower than men.[3] The lowest-paid jobs still are those traditionally done by women, such as carers, cleaners and child minders. This work is often unpaid.

Australia's Prime Minister Malcolm Turnbull hit the nail on the head in September, 2015, when he said: 'Disrespecting women does not always result in violence against women. But all violence against women begins with disrespecting women.'[4]

There are many ways in which domestic violence has been accepted and even encouraged over the centuries. This has not changed in many ways.

Some examples of serious gender inequality are forced marriage or female genital mutilation. Other common examples are lower rates of pay for work done by women or the belief that a man should be head of the household.

The oppression of women has a long history. Extreme gender violence is easy to see, and to condemn, such as the burning and drowning of 'witches' in medieval Europe; foot binding traditions in China that continued into the 20th century; 'honour killings' where a woman is murdered by a relative, and child marriages.

Female genital mutilation, which only recently became a human rights issue, has been forced upon at least 125 million girls in Africa and the Middle East, according to UNICEF.[5]

Female genital mutilation deprives girls of the right to control their own bodies or to experience sexual pleasure, and places them at risk of serious medical complications during childbirth.[6] Some oppression is less extreme, and less obvious, but will still seriously diminish a woman's independence and quality of life. These include restricting the opportunities for education and independent travel, having to accept less pay or not having reproductive rights. If anyone believes that these kinds of restrictions are justified, you can bet they will also justify other forms of oppression of women.

As the quote from Mr Turnbull implies, the oppression and abuse of women occurs on a continuum. While it is easy to condemn practices of the past (like foot binding), there are still many who do not identify that something as straightforward as workplace harassment is a form of violence against women which affects their freedom and wellbeing.

If a government minister, a senior politician running the country, propositions a workmate,[7] or a sports star propositions a reporter,[8] there are those who cannot see that this behaviour is wrong. They do not accept that it is inappropriate to put someone in that position, especially when they have so much more power in the situation because of their status. Instead we hear, 'It's just a joke, they're just being friendly, boys will be boys.'

There is a logical link between the belief that women are inferior in some way to men and the belief that men have a right to control women. Such beliefs are dangerous, and that is why gender inequity is also dangerous.

When I was growing up I had a great-aunt who was a teacher. She worked all her teaching life for 60 per cent of the wage that male teachers received.

She was a spinster and used to say to me that if there was a breadwinner in the house she could understand this disparity, but it seemed unfair to apply it to her because she had to pay the same as any man for her rent, her electricity or her loaf of bread.

Isn't it interesting that even for her, and even when she thought it unfair in her circumstances, she also accepted the justification of that era that women did not need to be paid equal pay for equal work if there was another breadwinner in the household?

People usually accept the status quo whether it is unequal pay, voting rights, foot binding or slavery.

These days in Australia, for instance, a large section of the population accepts offshore detention of asylum seekers, while others campaign about shockingly inhumane conditions, which Amnesty International[9] and the United Nations Refugee Agency have condemned.[10] It remains to be seen how Australians manage this issue in the future.

There comes a turning point, usually led by a few courageous people who question the status quo, where what was once acceptable is no longer accepted. I have seen this in my life-time in terms of gay liberation and the animal rights movements. Maybe we are at that turning point in relation to gender equity.

History and psychology

There are many ways in which society views women's lives differently from those of men. It is interesting to examine how such views have changed over the years, and how they affect everyday life.

Some aspects of society continue to contribute to the unequal status of men and women, to the detriment of both genders. The following examples are offered to show how theories, traditional and popular culture can make the world safer, or not, for women. The Age of Enlightenment and the Industrial Revolution engendered many new scientific discoveries. New theories about the world emerged that did not rely on religious texts, such as the discovery that the earth orbited the sun.

The Catholic Church rather famously responded quite badly to that discovery, seeing it as a challenge to their authority.[11]

Darwin's theory of evolution is another example of a theory that challenged dominant religious thinking.

Human rights began to be recognised, and this led to changes such as the abolition of slavery in America, the widening of educational opportunities, the introduction of child labour laws and changes to voting rights.

Along with these changes, some people were trying to find out what makes people tick, why humans think and behave as they do. My own profession is the study of behaviour, especially human behaviour. While interest in what makes people tick is as old as humanity, the professions of psychology and psychiatry (the study and treatment of mental illness) emerged as professions during the 20th century.

This growth was assisted, and some would say had its genesis, in the work and theories of Sigmund Freud, sometimes referred to as the father of psychiatry. Freud came up with some interesting concepts, such as the 'unconscious', and 'repression'. He is still regarded by many in the 'talking professions' as an important seminal thinker.

However, he did a grave disservice to those women who revealed to him that they had been molested, and in a real sense he betrayed the very women who came to him for help.

At first, when women confided to Freud that men in their network of family and friends had sexually assaulted them, he did something both understandable and commendable, he believed them! He was shocked, appalled and spoke out about this issue, because he worked out that they had difficulties and issues connected to the events they described, what we would today call childhood trauma. He started speaking publicly about this in 1896.[12] Not surprisingly, other men (doctors were almost all men at that time) took serious exception to this. He was in danger of being ostracised by the very men he was trying to impress. So, he changed his mind and his theory. He decided to say that his clients were not talking about real events; they were deluded, they were repressed, and they were really victims of their own sexual urges. He suggested that sometimes women feel guilty about their forbidden sexual urges, and even that they sometimes feel better if they are mistreated.

He theorised that there were mechanisms he called 'repression' and 'masochism' to explain reports of childhood abuse that he did not believe had occurred.[13]

He saw femininity as 'thwarted masculinity' and believed in a condition called 'hysteria' that only women experienced.[14]

Unfortunately for women, these theories were much more palatable to the men around Freud than the truth had been, and they opened up a whole new fertile field of victim blaming as well as a valuing of reason over emotion. Freud's ideas about sex and gender are thankfully now outdated and mostly discarded, so why is this all relevant?

He was, above all, a man of his times pursuing the chauvinist views held by most of society at that time.

The relevance is as an example of a prominent and influential theorist getting it wrong in relation to women, whose influential theories still can be argued to affect how women in distress are regarded. While the belief that emotional distress can lead to both psychological and physical symptoms still has validity, the dismissal of women's experiences or reports because of a distrust of emotionality has hampered progress in eradicating violence from women's lives.

Views that reflect this misrepresentation and are still prevalent include women not being believed or being blamed for 'taking' abuse, or for not leaving when they are being hurt.

Sometimes the dangerousness of the behaviour they are reporting is minimised, especially if they show ambivalence or hesitate about continuing the relationship.

If women are not believed then the abuser can continue to be abusive without suffering any consequences, especially if women or children are not believed in court. If a woman speaks about being sexually abused at home she may be regarded as mad or at least psychologically compromised.

While women may no longer be seen as responding to repressed urges, their reports of abuse are sometimes still seen as delusions that they have foisted upon their small child in a malicious attempt to prevent a father and child having contact. This is another way to refuse to believe victims, and can perpetuate the danger to the woman and the child.

Religion and culture

Many religions support the ascendancy or authority of men over women. I have met many women who live with abuse at home because leaving a marriage is 'against their religion' or because they believe, often correctly, they would be ostracised from their religious community if they did so.

Consider the Judeo/Christian Old Testament, which I grew up with. It is thought to have been written by men, and is claimed to be inspired by God. The first story in the Bible is about Adam and Eve, and when things go horribly wrong the first thing the man (Adam) does is to blame the woman (Eve).

Not only that, God decides that from then on 'man shall have dominion over woman'.

Well, that's convenient, at least for men. From then on the Old Testament relates countless examples of women being abused, bartered, sold and sexually assaulted as if this is all perfectly normal. While most people who practise a religion would not condone this behaviour, many of our laws and beliefs have been built on the notions of domination, ownership and distrust of women and this is still reflected in some community attitudes.

Generally, the more fundamentalist the practitioners of a religion, the more subjugated are the women in that religious community. This is important when we consider the recent research linking gender inequality with higher rates of violence against women. The most dangerous societies for women are those dominated by religious fundamentalism, where women can be beaten for wearing 'immodest' clothing or executed for being victims of rape or incest.[15]

Of course, in those same countries men are not subject to the same restrictions or consequences, even if they are responsible for sexual assault.[16]

Mara's story

Mara grew up in a religious family with a rich cultural heritage. There were two important things that she knew from an early age. The first was that her father was the boss, the head of the family, and his word was law. The second was that the family loved and believed in their religion and obeyed its laws. They often went to church.

When Mara was aged 12, her parents told her they had chosen her future husband. He was a well-off businessman and they were pleased that the marriage would honour her and the family. Her husband was aged 37. Mara was surprised; she had seen on television some romantic sitcoms and movies, and she was disappointed that she would have no say in choosing her life partner. She had not expected her future to be decided so soon, but as far as she knew her 20-year-old sister was happy in her arranged marriage. She was already an aunty to her sister's two children. In time, there was a traditional wedding and her husband gave her some beautiful jewellery, and some art supplies (her special request). Mara was proud to have such a handsome man as her husband, and his business was even more successful than her father's.

Unfortunately, her husband was very unlike her father in his conduct, and soon he was treating Mara as his servant. She could not meet his demands: she was not cleaning the house as he wanted, he scoffed at her cooking, and she was terrified of him in the bedroom. There were few days that did not end with her in tears. This infuriated him even more, he wanted to know what was wrong with her, and she wished she knew.

By the time she was 24, Mara had three children and was both used to her husband's cruelty and convinced he would kill her one day. He had threatened this often.

One night a neighbour called the police after hearing the screams of Mara and her children, and the police went to their house four times that year. Eventually, Mara ended up in hospital and confided to her sister the hell her life had become. With great difficulty, and in spite of her name being blackened in her community, Mara sought safety with her children.

It is vital to understand that intimate partner violence occurs in all cultures and communities. There is a complex relationship between the beliefs and attitudes someone grows up with in a family and their adult choices about how they treat others.

Many culturally and linguistically diverse and Indigenous groups are working very hard to challenge traditional views and educate people in their own communities, and they are the ones with the expertise in this area. I do not speak for them and I credit their insightful and courageous work. Governments need to engage with their efforts and fund local prevention, support and response programs that seek to keep women and children in diverse communities safe from family violence.

This book is not about how terrible other cultures are; we have too much of a problem in our own backyards to be pointing the finger. It is vital, though, that we recognise the connection between cultural or religious oppression of people and abuse in our own multi-cultural society.

Any culture — be it religious, political, ethnic or a community sub-culture — that promotes the idea that children are possessions, or that women are somehow inferior to men, or that men are more capable or entitled to decision-making roles, puts women and children at risk of exploitation and abuse.

Even a benevolent dictator is still a dictator. Any cultural belief that prizes one sex, race or spiritual belief over another is a fertile field for ignorance, discrimination and violence. Culture is no excuse for abuse.

Advertising and media

Perhaps you feel you are not affected by religion or by whatever Freud said about women. Let us look at something that affects everyone, how women are portrayed and treated in the media.

The media is a microcosm of modern culture, it both reflects and shapes how we view ourselves and others. It influences our expectations and our judgements.

As Naomi Wolf said, in *The Beauty Myth*: 'To live in a culture in which women are routinely naked where men aren't is to learn inequality in little ways all day long.'[17]

Some films show men arriving to rescue women, often to carry them off as a sort of prize, which Richard Gere does literally at the end of *An Officer and A Gentleman*.

They perpetuate the idea that women are weaker, more emotional and also that men are somehow entitled to a relationship with any woman they want. It teaches that pestering women with unwanted attention is part of courtship, and that when a woman has said 'no' she really means 'yes'.

This common 'romantic' theme, and the 'happily ever after' myth can blind us to warning signs of abuse in a relationship and perpetuate ideas of ownership of women as a right. These warning signs can be seen in the classic, Gone With The Wind, which has numerous examples of physical and emotional abuse that Rhett inflicts on Scarlett, including spanking and sexual assault, to the highly popular Fifty Shades of Grey, which is seen by those who work with and understand this issue as a film depicting some of the worst kinds of intimate partner abuse.[18,19]

In advertising, the use of images of scantily clad women to promote sales of an enormous range of products continues, from tyres (such as Ultratune's 'We're into rubber' campaign) to deodorant (Lynx). It extends at times to the use of implied sexual threat, such as the infamous pack rape images used by Dolce and Gabbana[20] and Calvin Klein.[21] The media frequently does men a grave disservice also, portraying them as being either insensitive brutes or incompetent to undertake domestic tasks.[22]

The media has a lot of power in the shaping of community attitudes. It is always heartening when it is used to promote positive community awareness and gender equality.[23]

Pornography

One increasing factor in the development of sexual standards and expectations is internet pornography. Pornography has, over recent decades, become more accessible and more hard core, which means it is usually both violent and degrading to women.

In an interview, quoted on the Domestic Violence Resource Centre website, a prize-winning male porn actor said: 'You have to be rough with the girl and take charge.'[24]

This is exactly the thinking of perpetrators of violence against women. It explains why pornography can be expected to have a negative impact on its viewers' attitudes to women, and to sexual consent. As a professional who works with victims of intimate partner violence, and having been involved in the development of a violence prevention program for schools, I find pornography a great concern. Young people's expectations of intimate relationships are being distorted in dangerous ways if violence and coercion are normalised.

Women in the world

One of the prevailing assumptions — I certainly believed it when I was growing up — is that the world is pretty much the same for men and women in terms of their freedom to operate in society.

It is not — the world is very different for women and the discussion about gender equality has highlighted some ways in which this is the case.

It seems incongruous to me that our society often accepts that women are unsafe in the community, but expects women to take steps to ensure their safety rather than restrict those who pose a danger.

In March, 2015, a 17-year-old girl, Masa Vukotic, was brutally murdered in a park in the Melbourne suburb of Doncaster.[25]

After this shocking crime a well-meaning detective was quoted as saying that females should not be alone in parks.[26]

He was accused of victim blaming, focusing on what women must do to protect themselves instead of stopping the crimes that men commit.

What are the facts? Are women safe in a park? Are they safe during the day but not at night? If they are not safe in parks, whose fault is that? What should be done?

What sort of things do men need to do every day to avoid being sexually assaulted? The usual answer to this is: nothing at all. By contrast, women take such frequent and practised actions to avoid assault that it is part of their daily routine.

Women have to make decisions about where they walk and when; where they park; whether they go out accompanied; whether they leave their ground floor windows open on a hot night; what they wear; who they feel safe to ask directions from, the list goes on.

This is sometimes referred to as 'rape culture'. Rape culture describes the ways in which society normalises male sexual violence and blames victims of sexual assault. To understand rape culture is to understand so much that is relevant to gender equality.

Rape culture describes the ways in which society normalises male sexual violence and blames victims of sexual assault.

It is transposed into beliefs such as men have the right to teach their partners a lesson; men should be head of the household, or that some women 'ask' or 'deserve' to be raped.

It includes such destructive beliefs as a man's right to fight when he believes his honour or status is challenged.

It is epitomised in 'honour killings'; in the way women are demeaned in advertising and pornography; in the way women are exhorted to behave, to dress, to speak and to stay home at night. It is the common acceptance that men will be violent, as if this is inevitable. How insulting for men! It is pervasive and dangerous. It can lead to violence being glamorised as not only sexy, but compulsory, as we have noted in the world of advertising and entertainment.

Think for a moment and reconsider the well-meaning detective who after the murder in Doncaster advised women to keep out of public parks. He could confidently suggest that women are not safe to walk in parks alone in case a man attacks them. What if he had said that it is a threat to community safety for men to walk in parks because they might attack women?

If the first suggestion seems somewhat sensible to you and the second a bit ridiculous then you have just demonstrated the power (and your acceptance) of rape culture.

My friend Stella

I was having a coffee with some old friends, Pam and Stella, and the topic turned to the case of a footballer who had been accused of rape after a night on the town. Stella and Pam have been friends of mine for decades, and Stella recently celebrated her 30th wedding anniversary to Tom.

She said she had some sympathy for young footballers, thrown into the limelight of fame and celebrity, and 'chased' by 'groupie' fans who just want to be part of their reflected glory. Stella pointed out that these young women can 'lead a man on' and get a young man excited, especially if they have both been drinking, and that it was unfair to call it rape if the girls had gone to his hotel room and had been canoodling.

The conversation moved to considering at what point it would be rape; when does sexual consent become immaterial? I asked her to imagine having sex with Tom, and asked when did sexual consent become immaterial to her? Is it OK for her to change her mind about having sex, even if they have just been out for dinner, or if they have already started to be intimate? Does it evaporate because she is already in bed, or he is already aroused? Stella admitted that even if they were in the act of making love, she could at any time reconsider and Tom would stop and understand. The notion that men are incapable of controlling their sexuality does a grave disservice to both sexes.

Rape culture is behind the pervasive insistence that false reports of rape are common, although they are less common (2.1 per cent)[27] than false reports of auto theft (2-10 per cent).[28]

It is the music of Eminem or Chris Brown; it is the smug expression of a man leaving court after having a charge of assaulting his partner dismissed and it is the excusing of sportsmen or celebrities who use violence. It is teaching girls how to say 'No' rather than teaching boys how to hear it.

What about us? We're not like that, are we? What do recent surveys of community attitudes in Australia tell us?

Community attitudes

Attitudes contribute towards violence against women, especially in their intimate relationships. They are shaped by our early influences and by media and popular culture.

In 2015, the Australian Government released the latest National Community Attitudes Towards Violence Against Women Survey.[29] There is good news and bad news. On the plus side, most Australians have some knowledge about violence against women and most do not support attitudes that endorse such violence.

However, only about two-thirds of people (68 per cent) believe that violence against women is common and this percentage has dropped from 74 per cent in 2009. I guess it depends on what you mean by 'common'.

When so many lives are being blighted, and with at least one murder as a result of intimate partner violence occurring weekly, it is clearly much too common.

To paraphrase a popular road toll campaign — what number would be acceptable?

The survey asked respondents to consider three possible 'causes' of domestic violence: and about two-thirds said that the main cause is men not being able to control their anger.

However, VicHealth finds that gender inequality is the cause with the highest level of supporting evidence.[30] The survey found that this factor, 'a belief that men should be in charge of the relationship' was chosen as a causal factor by fewer than 20 per cent of respondents.

Misinformed attitudes can help perpetrators escape consequences and continue to be abusive.

Community attitudes influence how we treat both victims and perpetrators, so it is important that the community is as well informed as possible. Such attitudes can make it easier for people to be victimised, less likely that they will seek help, and harder for them to find it. For example, 43 per cent of people who took this survey agreed with the statement: 'Rape results from men not being able to control their need for sex.' If this is true, why do only a minority of men commit rape?

The danger of such a belief is clear. If a man believes this, he may use it to excuse sexual assault. If a policeman believes this, he may be less likely to charge a man accused of rape. If a jury believes this then they may excuse the violence and blame the victim. If a magistrate believes this, the accused may receive a lighter sentence or not be convicted.

The victim, if she also carries this attitude, might not recognise the sexual assault, might excuse the rape or might feel partly responsible. In any case, this attitude encapsulates the idea that men are not to be held fully responsible for violent or coercive sexual behaviour. It is worrying that in 2009, only 35 per cent of respondents to the same question agreed with the above statement.

The Australian community is now less well informed than six years ago.

Other attitudes can minimise or trivialise violence such as believing that domestic violence is only a private matter, or that it is not serious if it is not physical violence.

These beliefs could affect, for instance, whether a person is considered to have breached an intervention order. If the breach does not involve physical contact or is not seen as serious enough for police to intervene, the perpetrator gets the message that they can get away with some form of harassment. It can influence whether a woman reports violence, if she does not expect it to be regarded as serious.

Another issue raised is that men may be less likely to report the domestic violence they experience than women. A study in 1998 found that men tend to overestimate their partner's violence while women underestimate their partner's violence by normalising or excusing it.[31]

I am sometimes told that violence towards men by women is not reported because men feel too much shame to disclose it. My experience is that women also feel enormous shame in being the victims of violence from their partner, and talking about it. I have not seen any evidence that they feel any less shame than male victims or that women generally get a better response from police than men who complain.

Furthermore, research consistently shows that men's (domestic) violence is six times more likely to inflict severe injury and is more humiliating, coercive and controlling.

Women are more likely to commit violence in response to frustration and stress, or to defend themselves, rather than purposefully with the intention to control and dominate.[32]

To maintain that domestic violence is a gender-equal crime is not merely incorrect, it is dangerous.

CHAPTER FIFTEEN

CHANGING THE WORLD

What can stop intimate partner violence?

What does stop intimate partner violence? Has there been real progress anywhere?

If you want an inspiring read, there is a book that chronicles a success story in America.

It is *The Quincy Solution* by Barry Goldstein.[1] Quincy is a city in Massachusetts, USA, that has been making real progress to reduce domestic violence for more than 30 years. Goldstein's book makes both sobering and inspiring reading.

Quincy, a county that used to average five to six domestic violence murders annually, has now experienced many years where there are no domestic violence murders at all. Their initiatives have been introduced to San Diego and Nashville, with similar results.

In summary, the Quincy model brought together law enforcement, court personnel and domestic violence workers to develop two main areas of best practice.

One is to develop a more responsive and reliable safety net for victims, and the other is to strictly enforce criminal law, protective orders and probation conditions.

These two arms of intervention require considerable understanding of intimate partner violence, and both a commitment and the resources to put them into effect — but they work. It really is that simple. The Quincy model will only work if police and courts both enforce the law as it should be enforced.

Only when perpetrators realise that there will be real consequences for the abuse they inflict, will they stop the abuse.

Amazingly, although the originators of the Quincy model were warned that the prison population would swell if it was pursued, four decades later not only are there fewer men in prison for domestic violence offences, Massachusetts now has one of the lowest rates of imprisonment in the USA.[2]

Perhaps this is partly due to a generation of Quincy children who have not grown up with domestic violence.

A local example of something that really works is the BSafe, or safety card program. This program, piloted by Women's Health Goulburn North East, provides women at risk with an electronic safety card.[3] Victims can wear this, like an employee card, and when activated it not only records what is happening, but can be linked to a support or security service that will respond immediately.

When these were first introduced, some domestic violence agencies were worried that perpetrators may become angrier and more dangerous, knowing their ex-partners had these cards. The opposite seems to have occurred. Once perpetrators know their behaviour will be recorded and a response will be swift, they stop harassing their ex-partners.[4]

A lot of progress has been made in supporting women and children over the last four decades in Australia. The situation is far from perfect, but there are many good services that assist thousands of women. In the current political climate they are paradoxically both inundated with clients and often under financial threat, especially those operating from smaller agencies, even though these provide excellent and innovative tailor-made services for their clients. Women's services all over are swamped by demand and grossly under resourced, but they are well informed and hold a great deal of expertise. The workers in this field are some of the most dedicated and courageous women I have ever met.

On the other hand, we have barely started when it comes to holding perpetrators to account. As discussed in preceding chapters, victims are frequently let down by the law, particularly the court outcomes. Until this changes, the incidence of domestic violence will continue unchecked. Goldstein, in The Quincy Solution,[5] writes at length about issues with the Family Courts in the USA that mirror those in Australia, and he notes the frequency with which dangerous perpetrators seek custody as a tactic to retain control over their victims, placing many children and their protective parents at great risk.

Where to from here?

This book may have answered some of your questions about domestic violence, and it has probably raised some others.

Hopefully, you have a better idea about what is meant by domestic violence and how people are affected by it. In order to reduce the number of people whose lives are damaged by domestic violence there need to be some big shifts in our collective thinking.

These can be summarised as:

- We tend to think of domestic violence as a series of unfortunate incidents experienced by an individual victim. Instead, domestic violence is a pattern of criminal behaviour by the one individual. We know who the individual is and that they are likely to abuse a series of victims over time, namely their partners and their children.

- We, as a society and our systems, tend to judge and blame survivors and hold them responsible for their own safety, and that of their children. Instead, domestic violence is the responsibility of the person doing the harm. It is they who hold their partners and children hostage in cruel and often brutal situations. It is they who must be held to account for the damage they cause. It is the perpetrator of abuse who must be responsible for positive change.

- It is important to recognise that children are also victims where domestic violence is occurring. A person who uses abuse and violence towards them or their mother or carer is not a safe parent. Using violence in the presence of children is a type of child abuse. We will know we are making progress when the onus for protecting these children is placed squarely on changing either the perpetrator's behaviour or their access to the children.

- Gradually the community is moving from a sense of a passive victim to an active survivor. Survivors spend an enormous amount of energy trying to stay safe. We need to celebrate and facilitate this resistance to violence. We need to make it as easy as possible for them by taking action against those who abuse their partners and children.

- Women who are survivors of intimate partner violence often believe they did too little to protect themselves. However, I am in awe of the various ways in which women have tried to keep themselves and their children safe, both within the relationship and after they have left. Such resistance might include teaching her children about staying safe, making sure she always knows where her car keys are, altering her routines to minimise stalking, or just telling herself that the abuse she is hearing is untrue or undeserved. Every measure taken by these women is an effort to retain their psychological integrity and personal dignity, and is valuable to their mental health and recovery.

- Domestic violence cannot be understood unless we appreciate that the world is different for men and women in terms of both safety and opportunity, which means that the world is different for men and women in terms of power. Men dominate the most powerful roles in politics, the law, religion, corporations and institutions. This puts women at a disadvantage in having the power and resources to be in charge of their own lives and to have an equally credible voice in the world. Women are less likely to use violence than men and they are most at risk of assault in their own homes, by someone they know and usually have loved.

How can we improve the system?

The solution lies in holding perpetrators to account and providing an effective safety net for victims. The solution includes the following realisations:

- If we accept that perpetrators are responsible for their decisions to use abuse and violence, and that victims are in a hostage type situation, then the community must take on the responsibility to help the victims achieve safety. The perpetrator usually won't and the victim usually can't. People who abuse their family members need to be held to account through a no-tolerance policy to violence and abuse. Consequences should be significant, and guaranteed.

- Meaningful consequences need to occur because perpetrators of abuse will change their behaviour only when it is not worth continuing to use it.

- We need to support victims without diminishing the victim's personal autonomy. It is the woman seeking help who needs to be in charge of the process and trusted, believed and supported to take whatever next steps she decides are right for her.

- The assessment of dangerousness is at least as important as the assessment of a victim's capacity to protect themselves or their children. Police and domestic violence services have great understanding of domestic violence, and should be part of assessing a partner and/or a parent's dangerousness.

- The system to support those affected by domestic violence is not effective, in fact it is not really a system. It is a series of agencies trying to help, with very constrained budgets and inadequate coordination across and within sectors.

- Agencies charged with protecting children, primarily Child Protection Services and the Family Court, must have the training and resources to investigate allegations of abuse against children and their primary carers. This can equip them to recognise that the best predictor of future behaviour is past behaviour and where there has been dangerous behaviour, they must demand evidence that such behaviour has changed.

- Currently each Australian state has different approaches to this issue, and different support structures and legalities. Such anomalies make it harder for women and children to seek and maintain safety, and can make it all the more difficult for women when they reach the Family Court. However, there is legislative work being done so that protective orders in one state are enforceable across Australia.[6]

- Education is always needed to inform the community about the prevalence and dynamics of intimate partner violence and to dispel the myths about it.

How can everyone help?

There are many ways everyone can help; they are all simple, and some are courageous.

Be aware of sexism and refuse to accept or condone it. This might be a greater awareness about sexist remarks or sexist jokes, and calling them out. If you are a man, it might mean doing your share of caring and domestic chores, in order to live a life of equality. If you are a woman it might entail offering support rather than judgement to a friend who makes a disclosure about domestic abuse.

For all of us, it can consist of checking a tendency to judge a woman rather than a man when a relationship is in trouble. It means having real conversations with friends about issues like rape or harassment, or the way women are portrayed in advertising.

It might mean not discouraging your son from crying when he is hurt, not perpetuating disparaging views of women by calling him 'a girl' if he shows emotion. If you tell your son to 'be a man' make sure you are encouraging an equitable and fair concept of masculinity.

It might mean gently checking that someone you are worried about it is OK and telling them you will always be there to help if they need it, and meaning it no matter how long that takes. I think you get the picture. Fundamentally, it means supporting all victims and not accepting that violence against women is inevitable, or that men are inevitably violent.

As I write this, the Victorian Royal Commission into Family Violence has just handed down its report. I congratulate all those involved in the process and welcome it with open arms.

I hope that governments to come have the courage and commitment to finally put the resources into addressing this issue, especially into front line services. So much needs to be done.

It was Mahatma Gandhi who said: 'If we could change ourselves, the tendencies in the world would also change. As a man changes his own nature, so does the attitude of the world change towards him ... We need not wait to see what others do.'

This is often re-phrased as 'Be the change you want to see in the world' but I like the original (although I would replace 'man' with 'someone'). Change yourself first, now that you have had some of your questions answered, and the attitude of the world will change ever so slightly.

If you want to make a practical difference, donate to a domestic violence charity such as the Luke Batty Foundation[7] or the Dorothy Rose Fund[8] or to an op shop that supports services for those who have lived with violence.

If you are living with violence, try to find someone to talk to that you can trust. Take a step to safety. Finally, if you have been violent or controlling within your family, get help, get it fast, and do whatever it takes to ensure you are safe to be around; because your life will be so much richer when you do. In any group you are with, at least a quarter of the women and at least a sixth of the men will have experienced violence within their family, as a child or as an adult. Family violence does not affect others, it affects us: our children, our workmates, our neighbours, our extended family.

Intimate partner violence diminishes us all. You will inevitably be a bystander, try to be brave enough to offer to help, to encourage others to support rather than judge, and to point out faulty attitudes and sexist responses.

You will then be more than a bystander, you will be standing up for women, for children and for men.

RESOURCES

International resources

www.hotpeachpages.net

HotPeachPages is an international directory of domestic violence agencies. This website provides links to family violence services in countries across the world, in a range of languages.

Australian resources

These resources provide information about family violence and links to services. To locate local services, call your local community health service or police station.

24 Hour call centre: 1800 737 732
On line: www.1800respect.org.au
Kids Helpline: 1800 55 1800

Other helpful websites:

www.loveisrespect.org www.breakthecycle.org
www.burstingthebubble.com
www.respect.gov.au www.dvirc.org.au

Smartphone apps:
Australian

- LiveFree — general information about IPV and direct links to national and Victorian services
- Aurora — general information about IPV, major services and a special messaging service to friends for help
- Daisy — links to support services
- iMatter — sharing app for info about healthy relationships; engaging Appforyoungpeople

USA

- *Domestic Violence Information* — similar to LiveFree and Aurora, released in the USA so has phone numbers for all US states.

REFERENCES

Chapter One

1. Literature review on domestic violence perpetrators, September, 2013, Urbis, <www.dss.gov.au/sites/default/files/documents/09_2013/literature_review_on_domestic_vi olence_perpetrators.pdf >

2. A summary of the latest published research examining violence against women in Australia and its prevention, 19 October, 2011, VicHealth <www.vichealth.vic.govagainst-women-in-australia-research-summary>

3. Violence against Australian women key statistics, Accessed: May, 2016, < anrows.org. au/ sites/default/files/Violence-Against-Australian-Women-KeyStatistics.pdf>

4. Straus, Murray A. February, 1979. 'Measuring intra-family conflict and violence: The Conflict Tactics (CT) Scales' (PDF). *Journal of Marriage and the Family* 41 (1): pp. 75–88.

5. Measuring domestic violence and sexual assault against women. EBrief: Online only issued 6 December, 2004, updated 12 December, 2006. Accessed: May, 2016. <www.aph.gov.au/about_parliament/parliamentary_departments/ parliamentarylibrary/publicationsarchive/archive/violenceagainstwomen>

6. Family Violence and Sexual Assault Unit, Department of Justice. Victorian Family Violence Database Vol <www.victimsofcrime. vic.gov.au/utility/for+professionals/research+reports/victorian+-family+violence+database+volume+5+elevenyear+trend+analysis+19 99-2010>

7. Cussen, Tracey, and Bryant, Willow., May, 2015, *Domestic/family homicide in Australia* Australian Institute of Criminology. <www. aic. gov.au/publications/current%20series/rip/21-40/rip38.html>

8. Australian Bureau of Statistics Personal Safety Survey 2012 Issued December 2013 <www.ausstats.abs.gov.au/Ausstats/

subscriber.nsf/0/056A404DAA576AE6CA2571D00080E985/$-
File/49060_2005%20(reissue).pdf>

9. PricewaterHouseCoopers, *A high price to pay: the economic case
    for preventing violence against women*, November, 2015 <www.
    pwc.com.au/publications/economic-case-preventing-vio-
    lence-against-women.html>

10. Blumer, Clare, Australian Broadcasting Commission. Australian
    police deal with a domestic violence matter every two minutes.
    5 June, 2015. <www.abc.net.au/news/2015-05-29/domestic-vio-
    lence-data/6503734>

11. Groombridge, Nic. *How many times women assaulted before re-
    porting to police?* Criminology in Public. March, 2014. <criminolo-
    gyinpublic.blogspot.com.au/2014/03/how-many-times-women-
    assaulted-before.html>

Chapter Two

1. American Psychiatric Association. 1994. Fact Sheet: Violence and
    Mental Illness. Washington, DC: American Psychiatric Associa-
    tion.

2. American Psychiatric Association. 2013, *Diagnostic and statistical
    manual of mental disorders,* 5th edn, Arlington, VA: American
    Psychiatric Publishing.

3. Taft, A, and Wilson, I. 2015, *Alcohol's role in domestic violence,*
    Latrobe University. Accessed: 1 July, 2016, <www.latrobe.edu.
    au/news/articles/2015/ opinion/alcohols-role-in-domestic-vio-
    lence>

4. Abramsky, T., Watts, C., Garcia-Moreno, C., Devries, K., Kiss, L., &
    Ellsberg, M. et al. 2011, *What factors are associated with recent
    intimate partner violence?* Findings from the WHO multi-country
    study on women's health and domestic violence. BMC Public
    Health, 11(1), p. 109. <dx.doi.org/10.1186/1471-2458-11-109>

5. UNICEF and The Body Shop International, *Behind Closed Doors:
    the impact of domestic violence on children*, 2006, London, UK

6. Atmore, Chris, 2001, *Men as victims of domestic violence: some issues to consider*. Discussion Paper No 2. Melbourne: Domestic Violence and Incest Resource Centre.

7. Carlson, K., and Mulder, L., *Family and domestic violence: a gendered crime*, 2009, (with permission)

8. 'I want to tell people that family violence happens to [anybody], no matter how nice your house is, no matter how intelligent you are.' Rosie Batty, speaking on 14 February, 2014, two days after her son was murdered by his father. <www. abc.net.au/news/2015-01-26/rosie-batty-quotes/6046216>

9. *The ethics of bravery: why a Black Saturday 'hero' lost his award*, June, 2012, The Conversation. Accessed: 6 July, 2016, from <the-conversation.com/the-ethics-of-bravery-why-a-blacksaturday-hero-lost-his-award-7794>

10. Father at centre of Story Bridge tragedy was teacher at exclusive school. February, 2012, www.news.com.au, Accessed: 6 July, 2016, from <www.news.com.au/national/avoid-story-bridge-on-monday-commute/story-e6frfkwr-1226275439857>

11. Lockhart shootings: Handwritten note saying 'I'm sorry' found in home of NSW family killed in shooting, inquest to hear. 2015, ABC News. Accessed: 6 July, 2016, from <http://www.abc.net. au/news/2015-10-06/inquest-into=hunt-family-murder-suicidebegins-in-nsw/68238666

12. Community 'gutted and distraught' after dad drives kids off wharf. 2016, ABC news. Accessed: 6 July, 2016, from <www.abc. net. au/news/2016-01-05/port-lincoln-in-shock-after-father-drives-car-off-wharf/7067272>

Chapter Three

1. Dimitri the stud, 2008, YouTube. Accessed: 6 July, 2016, from <www.youtube.com/watch?v=uRdmgDbswrl>

Chapter Four

1. UN Treaties on Domestic Violence. Oct, 2012, Stopvaw.org. Accessed: 6 July, 2016, from <www.stopvaw.org/un_treaties_ and_conventions>

2. Response Based Practice, 2016, Response Based Practice. Accessed: 6 July, 2016, from <www.responsebasedpractice.com>

3. Facts About Animal Abuse & Domestic Violence, 2016, Americanhumane.org. Accessed: 6 July, 2016, from <www.american-humane.org/interaction/support-the-bond/fact-sheets/ ani-mal-abuse-domestic-violence.html>

4. Common Risk Assessment Framework, 2008, Tafe.swinburne. edu.au. Accessed: 6 July, 2016, from <www.tafe.swinburne.edu. au/CRAF/manual.htm>

5. Victims of Crime Stalking Fact Sheet, 2012, Accessed: 6 July 2016, from <www.victimsofcrime.org/docs/src/stalking-fact-sheet_ english.pdf>

6. Cooper, A., 4 April, 2016, Teresa Mancuso expressed fears about ex-husband hours before death, court told, *The Age*

7. Gardiner, S., 12 May, 2015 Christopher Cullen murder trial told 'he had threatened to slit his wife's throat'. *The Sydney Morning Herald*

8. Campo, M., 2015, *Domestic Violence in pregnancy and early parenthood: Overview and emerging interventions*, Australian Institute of Family Studies, Commonwealth of Australia.

Chapter Five

1. Bancroft, Lundy, 2003, *Why Does He Do That: Inside the Minds of Angry and Controlling Men*, Penguin

2. From the 1944 film *Gaslight*, starring Ingrid Bergman. 'Gaslighting' refers to psychological abuse where someone causes their partner to doubt their own memory or reality. An example would be to move things around, such as furniture or car keys, then deny they have been moved.

3. Marital rape, 24 June, 2016, Wikipedia, The Free Encyclopedia. Accessed: 6 July, 2016, from <en.wikipedia.org/w/index.php?title=Marital_rape&oldid=726838185>

4. Marital rape, 24 June, 2016, Wikipedia, The Free Encyclopedia. Accessed: 6 July, 2016, from <en.wikipedia.org/w/index.php?title=Marital_rape&oldid=726838185>

Chapter Six

No references

Chapter Seven

1. Richards, K., June, 2011, *Children's exposure to domestic violence in Australia,* Australian Institute of Criminology. Accessed: 24 June, 2016, from <www.aic.gov.au/publications/current%20series/tandi/401-420/tandi419.html>

2. Family violence and children, 2015, Better Health Channel. Accessed: 6 July, 2016, from <www.betterhealth.vic.gov.au/ health/ healthyliving/domestic-violence-and-children>

3. Cunningham, A., and Baker, L., 2007, *Little Eyes, Little Ears,* Centre for children and families in the justice system. National Clearing House on Family Violence. Ontario

4. Batty Rosie, with Corbett, Bryce, 2015, *A Mother's Story,* Harper Collins

5. Lauder, S., 3 February, 2016, Domestic Violence victims make up 36% of demand for homelessness services, ABC News. Accessed: 5 May, 2016, < www.abc. net.au/news/2016-02-03/link-between-domestic-violence-andhomelessness/7135364>

6. Perkins, M., 28 July, 2015, The hidden toll: family violence linked to suicide deaths, *The Age*

7. Forsythe, L. & Adams, K., 2009, Mental health, abuse, drug use and crime: does gender matter? Canberra: Australian Institute of Criminology.

8. Gutierres, S.E., & Van Puymbroeck, C., 2006, Childhood and adult violence in the lives of women who misuse substances. Aggression and Violent Behavior, 11(5)

9. Family violence and children, 2015, Better Health Channel. Accessed: 6 July, 2016, from <www.betterhealth.vic.gov.au/ health/ healthyliving/domestic-violence-and-children>

10. Stockley, C., 2016, The role of out-of-home-care in criminal justice outcomes | Insight. Accessed: 6 July, 2016, from http:// insight.vcoss.org.au/the-role-of-out-of-home-care-in-criminal-justice-outcomes

11. Sisters Inside: Who Are Women Prisoners? (undated) accessed at <webcache.googleusercontent.com/search?q=cache:4IAzWBZ-MvNgJ: www.sistersinside.com.au/ media/housing.doc>

12. Campo, M., December, 2015, *Children's exposure to domestic and family violence: Key issues and responses*, Australian Institute for Family Studies CFCA Paper No. 36. Commonwealth of Australia

Chapter Eight

1. Australians attitudes to violence against women, 2014, vichealth. vic.gov.au Retrieved: 3 July, 2016, from <www.vichealth.vic.gov. au/media-and-resources/publications/2013national-community-attitudes-towards-violence-against-womensurvey>

Chapter Nine

1. Super Bowl 2015: Domestic Violence PSA. (2016), YouTube. Retrieved: 7 July, 2016, from <www.youtube.com/watch?v=5Z_zWIVRIWk>

2. Common Risk Assessment Framework. (2008), Tafe.swinburne. edu.au. Retrieved: 6 July, 2016, from <www.tafe.swinburne.edu. au/CRAF/manual.htm>

Chapter Ten

1. Livingstone, J., 2009, Have You Stopped Killing Your Spouse? - Sociological Images. Thesocietypages.org. Accessed: 7 July, 2016, from <thesocietypages.org/socimages/2009/04/26/guest-post-have-you-stopped-killing-your-spouse>

2. Psychology Today staff, P., updated 2016, Fatal Attraction, *Psychology Today*, Accessed: 7 July 2016, from <www.psychologyto-day.com/articles/199303/fatal-attraction>

Chapter Eleven

1. Knaus, C., 27 April, 2016, Treatment of domestic violence victims under fire, *The Canberra Times*

2. Ireland, J., 1 May, 2015, Domestic violence calls go unanswered as demand spikes, *The Sydney Morning Herald*

3. Technology safety | Domestic Violence Resource Centre Victoria. (2016), Dvrcv.org.au. Accessed: 7 July, 2016, from <www.dvrcv.org.au/knowledge-centre/technology-safety>

4. NSW Bureau of Crime Statistics and Research, 2010, Factors which influence the sentencing of domestic violence offenders, NSW

5. Royal Commission into Family Violence (2016), Royal Commission into Family Violence Submissions. Melbourne: Government of Victoria. Accessed at www.rcfv.com.au

Chapter Twelve

1. Family Court of Australia, 2014, Annual Report 2013-14 Part 3: Report of Court Performance, Government of Australia

2. Weber, David., 18 April, 2016, National Legal Aid calls for more funding after new figures reveal domestic violence a factor in 79pc of family law cases, ABC News. Accessed: 6 July, 2016, from <http://www.abc.net.au/news/2016-04-18/domestic-violence-a-factor-in-79pc-of-family-law-cases:-audit/7333368>

3. Hill, J., 2015, Suffer the Children: trouble in family court, *The Monthly*. Accessed from <https://www.themonthly.com.au/issue/2015/november/1446296400/jess-hill/suffer-children>

4. Alexander, H., 2013, False abuse claims are the new court weapon, retiring judge says, *The Sydney Morning Herald*. Accessed from <www.smh.com.au/national/false-abuse-claims-are-the-new-court-weapon-retiring-judge-says-20130705-2phao.html>

5. Caldwell, A., 2014, Domestic violence support networks say Family Court should do more to protect women, ABC Radio. Accessed: 6 July, 2016, from <www.abc.net.au/pm/content/2014/s4013350.htm>

6. Caldwell, A., 2014, Domestic violence support networks say Family Court should do more to protect women, ABC Radio. Accessed: 6 July, 2016, from <www.abc.net.au/pm/content/2014/s4013350.htm>

7. Fehlberg, B. and Milleard, May, 2015, Family violence and financial outcomes after parental separation, Australian Institute of Family Studies. Commonwealth of Australia

8. Patrick R., Cook K., and Taket A., 2007, Multiple barriers to obtaining child support: experiences of women leaving violent partners, Just policy: a journal of Australian social policy, Volume 45, pp. 21-29

9. University of Warwick, NSPCC, University of Roehampton, 2012, Domestic Violence, Child Contact, Post separation Violence. NSPCC, UK

10. McInnes, E., 2004, Keeping Children Safe: The links between family violence and poverty. Because Children Matter: Tackling Poverty Together, Uniting Missions National Conference, Adelaide

11. Fish, Ellen., 2009, Bad Mothers and Invisible Fathers: Parenting in the context of domestic violence. Discussion Paper No. 7. Melbourne: Domestic Violence and Incest Resource Centre

12. In the child's best Interests, 2015, Radio National. Accessed: 6 July, 2016, from <http://www.abc.net.au/radionational/>

programs/ backgroundbriefing/in-the-child's-best-inter-
ests-v2/6533660>

13. American Psychiatric Association, 2013, *Diagnostic and statistical manual of mental disorders*, 5th edn, Arlington, VA, American Psychiatric Publishing

14. Australians attitudes to violence against women, 2014, vichealth. vic.gov.au, Accessed: 3 July, 2016, from <https://www.vichealth. vic.gov.au/media-and-resources/publications/2013nation- al-community-attitudes-towards-violence-against-womensur- vey>

15. Meier, J., 2011, Parental Alienation Syndrome & Parental Aliena- tion: Research Reviews. National Resource Centre on Domestic Violence.Accessed: 6 July, 2016, from <http://www.vawnet. org/advancedsearch/printdocument.php?doc_id=1679&find_ type=web_desc_AR>

16. Goddard, J., 2015, Neither Seen Nor Heard: Australia's Child Pro- tection Conundrum, Family Law Express, Accessed: 6 July, 2016, at <journal/research/neither-seen-nor-heardaustralias-childpro- tection-conundrum/21/>

17. Meier, Joan S., 2009, A Historical Perspective on Parental Aliena- tion Syndrome and Parental Alienation, *Journal of Child Custody*, 6(3), 232– 257.

18. Ramos, N. and Allen, E., 30 January, 2016, State fumbled for an- swers while girl was in limbo, *The Boston Globe*

19. Overington, C., 21 November, 2009, Children must see dad, like it or not: Family Court, *The Australian*

20. Berkovic, N., 16 December, 2015, Family Court gives custody to dad despite 'sex abuse' claims, *The Australian*

21. Kirkwood, D., 2012, Just Say Goodbye: Parents who kill their children in the context of separation, Discussion Paper No 8, Melbourne: Domestic Violence and Incest Resource Centre.

22. The Doncare Angels for Women Network (DAWN) is a program conducted by the Doncaster Community Care and Counselling

Centre (Doncare), More information can be found at <https://doncare.org.au/the-dawn-program> Accessed: 6 July, 2016

Chapter Thirteen

No references

Chapter Fourteen

1. UNFPA United Nations Population Fund, 2008, Promoting gender equality: Frequently asked questions about gender. New York: UNFPA. Retrieved from <www.unfpa.org/gender/resources_faq.htm>. World Health Organisation. (2005), WHO multi-country study on women's health and domestic violence against women: Summary report of initial results on prevalence, health outcomes and women's responses. Geneva: WHO.

2. UNFPA United Nations Population Fund. (2008), Promoting gender equality: Frequently asked questions about gender. New York: UNFPA. Retrieved from <www.unfpa.org/gender/resources_faq.htm>.World Health Organization. (2005), WHO multi-country study on women's health and domestic violence against women: Summary report of initial results on prevalence, health outcomes and women's responses. Geneva: WHO. World Health Organization. (2010), Preventing intimate partner and sexual violence against women: Taking action and generating evidence. Geneva: WHO/London School of Hygiene and Tropical Medicine

3. Australian Government Workplace Gender Equality Agency. Gender Pay Gap Statistics <www.wgea.gov.au/sites/default/files/Gender_Pay_Gap_Factsheet.pdf >

4. Ireland, Judith., 24 September, 2015, Malcolm Turnbull's scathing attack on men who commit domestic violence, *The Sydney Morning Herald*

5. September 24, 2015. UNICEF 2013, pp. 3–26. *For Iraqi Kurdistan, also see Yasin, Berivan A. et al. 'Female genital mutilation among Iraqi Kurdish women: a cross-sectional study from Erbil city', BMC Public Health, 13 September, 2013. *For more information on

UNICEF's data collection, see 'Multiple Indicator Cluster Survey (MICS)', UNICEF, 25 May, 2012

6. WHO, New study shows female genital mutilation exposes women and babies to significant risk at childbirth. Accessed: 2 July, 2016, Whoint. 2016. <www.who.int/mediacentre/news/releases/2006/pr30/en/>

7. Bourke L., 29 December, 2015, Cities Minister Jamie Briggs quits Turnbull Government after 'incident' abroad, *The Sydney Morning Herald*

8. Thomsen S., 5 January, 2016, Chris Gayle hit on a journalist live on TV and it reveals a big problem with harassment, *Business Insider Australia*

9. Amnesty International, The Truth about Manus Island: 2013 report. Accessed: 30 June, 2016, available at <www.amnesty.org.au/images/uploads/about/ Amnesty_International_Manus_Island_report.pdf>

10. UNHCR UN Refugee Agency UNHCR Calls for Immediate Movement of Refugees and Asylum-Seekers to Humane Conditions. Accessed: 30 June, 2016, available at <unhcr.org.au/news/unhcr-callsimmediate-movement-refugees-asylum-seekers-humaneconditions/>

11. Marcus, Michael., 10 September, 2007, 1992 Catholic Church apologises to Galileo who died in 1642. Accessed: 30 June, 2016, available at <4thefirsttime.blogspot.com.au/2007/09/1992-catholic-churchapologizes-to.html>

12. Klett, Susan A., Rachman, Arnold W., 2015, *Analysis of the Incest Trauma: Retrieval, Recovery, Renewal*, Karnac Books Ltd

13. Freud, Sigmund, *Introductory Lectures on Psychoanalysis* (PFL 1) p. 414, 'These scenes from infancy are not always true. Indeed, they are not true in the majority of cases, and in a few of them they are the direct opposite of the historical truth.'

14. Freud, Sigmund, Breuer, Josef, 1895, *Studies on Hysteria*

15. The New Economy, 2014, 10 of the most dangerous countries to be a woman. Accessed: 2 July, 2016, from <www.theneweconomy.com/insight/10-of-the-most-dangerous-countries-to-be-a-woman>

16. Gali, Alicia, Wikipedia. Accessed: 2 July, 2016, from <en.wikipedia.org/wiki/Alicia_Gali>

17. Wolf, Naomi, 1990, *The Beauty Myth: How Images of Beauty Are Used Against Women*, Chatto &Windus

18. Westen, J-H, and Hawkins, D., 16 February, 2015, Fifty Shades of Grey will lead to spike of abuse in women, CNS News. Accessed: 30 June 2016, from <cnsnews.com/commentary/john-henry-westen/fifty-shadesgrey-will-lead-spike-abuse-women>

19. Aker, Angie, 14 February, 2015, Real quotes from 'Fifty Shades' that could make you rethink how you feel about it. Accessed: 2 July, 2016, from <www. upworthy.com/6-real-quotes-from-fifty-shades-that-could-makeyou-rethink-how-you-feel-about-it >

20. Dolce & Gabbana under fire AGAIN for gang rape ad, 2015, Mail Online. Accessed: 2 July, 2016, from <www.dailymail.co.uk/news/article-2999045/Dolce-Gabbana-fire-just-days-referring-children-born-IVF-synthetic-critics-discover-ad-depicts-woman-gang-raped.html>

21. Calvin Klein ads banned for promoting rape, *AdWeek*. Accessed: 2 July, 2016, from <www. adweek.com/adfreak/calvin-klein-ads-banned-promotingrape-12033>

22. The 'Dumb Dad' and the Domestic Commercial, YouTube. Accessed: 2 July, 2016, from <www.youtube.com/watch?v=DOGdgvbX5Ls>

23. Always #LikeAGirl. YouTube. Accessed: 2 July, 2016, from <www.youtube.com/watch?v=XjJQBjWYDTs>

24. Eroticising inequality: technology, pornography and young people | Domestic Violence Resource Centre Victoria, 2010, Dvrcv.org.au. Accessed: 2 July, 2016, from <www.dvrcv.org.au/ knowledge-centre/our-blog/eroticising-inequality-technologypornography-and-young-people>

25. Bachelard, M., 17 August, 2015, Masa Vukotic was stabbed 49 times by Sean Price, *The Age*

26. Calligeros, Marissa, 20 March, 2015, Parks not safe for women, says homicide squad boss, *The Age*

27. Heenan, Melanie, Murray, Suellen, 2006, Study of Reported Rapes in Victoria 2000-2003, Summary Research Report. Office of Women's Policy, State of Victoria

28. Rojas, P., Motor Vehicle Theft and Insurance Fraud. Accessed: 3 July, 2016, from <rostroncarlyle.com/article/motor-vehicle-theft-insurance-fraud/>

29. Australians' attitudes to violence against women, 2014, vichealth.vic.gov.au. Accessed: 3 July, 2016, from < www. vichealth.vic. gov.au/media-and-resources/publications/2013national-community-attitudes-towards-violence-against-womensurvey>

30. Our Watch, Australia's National Research Organisation for Women's Safety (ANROWS and VicHealth, ANROWS: Change the story: A shared framework for the primary prevention of violence against women and their children in Australia. Our Watch, Melbourne

31. Dobesh, R., et al, 1998, Separate and Intersecting Realities: A Comparison of Men's and Women's Accounts of Violence in Violence Against Women, Volume 4, No. 4

32. Atmore, Chris, 2001, Men as victims of domestic violence: some issues to consider. Discussion Paper No. 2. Melbourne: Domestic Violence and Incest Resource Centre

Chapter Fifteen

1. Goldstein, Barry, 2014, *The Quincy Solution, Stop Domestic Violence and save $500 billion*, Robert D Reed Publishers, Oregon

2. Horowitz, E., 15 January, 2015, If crime is falling, why aren't prisons sinking? *The Boston Globe*

3.   WHGNE, BSafe Project improving safety for vulnerable women and children escaping violence. Whealth.com.au. Accessed: 7 July, 2016, from <www.whealth.com.au/work_bsafe.html>

4.   Domestic violence 'safety card' trial proves successful, in the child's best interests, May, 2015, Radio National. Accessed: 6 July, 2016, at <www. abc.net.au/ radionational/programs/back-groundbriefing/in-thechild's-best-interests-v2/6533660>

5.   Lee, J. and Wroe, D., 5 November, 2015, Move to enforce family violence intervention orders across Australia, *The Sydney Morning Herald*

6.   The Luke Batty Foundation was established in February, 2014, after Luke Batty was killed by his father at cricket practice in Tyabb, Victoria, to help women and children affected by the trauma of family violence.

7.   The Dorothy Rose Fund is an initiative of Doncare, which provides small grants to women to help them become safe, stay safe or to aid their recovery.

ACKNOWLEDGEMENTS

I have so many people to thank for helping to bring this book into being.

Thank you to my many colleagues, especially those who read drafts of the manuscript. Special thanks to Heather, Irene, Sue, Robyn, Doreen and Karen for sharing your amazing clinical wisdom and experience. Thank you for your valuable insights and for challenging and expanding my thinking. Thank you to all the staff and volunteers at Doncare who have shown me such encouragement. I am inspired also by many colleagues in other organisations who face a tide of misery every day with amazing dedication and skill.

Many of my wonderful friends have helped nurture this book. I thank particularly my good friends Carolin and Maureen, who offered me their astute common sense as I wrote. While some friends smiled politely when I said I would write a book, my friend Angela simply said, 'I have never known you not to achieve whatever you set your mind to.' She is probably unaware how much that vote of confidence helped get me started.

This book would not be possible without the knowledge and understanding I have gained through my relationships with many hundreds of women and children over the last few decades. They are my real inspiration, and have taught me a thousand ways to face injustice and terror with dignity, courage and sheer nerve.

I am indebted to Annie Hall, my publisher, and her team for having faith in this book and for the painstaking care with which they have brought it to fruition. Annie took on an unknown author writing about a difficult subject with great passion and skill, and turned what would have been a self-published amateur effort into a truly professional script.

Finally, I owe an enormous debt to my family, to my husband, my children, and their partners and to my grandchildren. Their support and patience, their honesty and practicality, their laughter and love always sustain me.

CPSIA information can be obtained
at www.ICGtesting.com
Printed in the USA
LVOW11s2306081116
512210LV00001B/80/P